Praise for *Feed the Wolf: Befriending Our Fears in the Way of Saint Francis*

"In *Feed the Wolf* Jon Sweeney enables Francis, this thirteenth-century saint, to speak to us anew. This book is not just something you read; it is something you put into practice. And when we apply the wisdom of Saint Francis, it has the power not only to heal us but, through us, to heal a hurting world."

—Adam Bucko, coauthor of *Occupy Spirituality* and *New Monasticism*

"Sweeney's *Feed the Wolf* takes us deeper into the stories of St. Francis, offering us inspiration to move our heart and hands away from fear and comfort, and toward listening and gentleness."

—Shemaiah Gonzalez, storyteller and essayist

"Jon Sweeney has written several remarkable books about Saint Francis, but this one seems especially appropriate for these troubling times. Read this book, then read it again, and a few more times, and tell every open-hearted soul you know to buy a copy. It's that good."

—Claudia Love Mair, author of *Zora & Nicky* and *Don't You Fall Now*

"The mysteries of faith and creation undergird Jon Sweeney's scholarship and erudition. His fascination with the saint of Assisi provides a reliable guide for redemptive living."

—Thomas Lynch, author of *Bone Rosary: New and Selected Poems* and *The Depositions: New and Selected Essays on Being and Ceasing to Be*

FEED THE WOLF

FEED

BEFRIENDING OUR FEARS

THE

IN THE WAY OF SAINT FRANCIS

WOLF

JON M. SWEENEY

BROADLEAF BOOKS
MINNEAPOLIS

For Frederic and Mary Ann,
who helped pave the way,
and for future generations
who go looking for it.

CONTENTS

CONTENTS

PREFACE

He knew poets and musicians, soldiers and generals, mothers and fathers, merchants and travelers, sea captains and sultans. He knew rulers and fools, popes and court entertainers, cardinals and criminals, and lovers.

Francis of Assisi's life was the stuff of legend. People were even calling him a saint while he was still living, not because of any supernatural performances or special revelations from the Divine, but because, to use the language of a beautiful song by Sarah McLachlan, Francis lived a life filled with more "ordinary miracles."

Each chapter of this book illustrates those ordinary miracles, providing a context for his life. Each chapter offers brief episodes of conversation that create a kind of oral history by imagining people who usually have no voice in the record of his life but who we know were there, talking about him. These voices appear in *italics* in the middle of each chapter, like a chorus.

The nature of ordinary miracles is that they can be repeated.

Francis's eight-hundred-year-old path began as the way of Jesus made tangible in the thirteenth century, and I wouldn't be writing about it if I didn't believe it remains the surest way for a person today to turn away from fear and find grace in modern life.

January 23, 2021
Feast of Saint Marianne Cope of Moloka'i

INTRODUCTION

I take comfort in the witness of the ancient white pine. Many years of walking in the woods of Vermont and Wisconsin gathering firewood have taught me how a white pine can stand ninety feet tall or more, and every other branch, at any given time, may be dead.

If I fix my grip on the right low-hanging limb, its dry wood cracks easily with a strong pull. You don't see this in a maple, which lives wholly, every branch blooming with leaves each new spring, until it doesn't anymore. When one offshoot of the maple tree dies, the whole tree soon will perish. But not the towering white pine; it has the ability to accommodate death and keep returning year after year for a century or more.

Like every other human being who has been on this planet for a half-century or more, I have experienced suffering and failure and death.

I used to think I was lucky, that the big events had passed me by. I was, and they did. But as you grow older there is a slow-dripping accumulation, like the gradual wearing away of cavern rock, that begins to feel like water rising around your ankles. Mentors die; a marriage ends; you witness friends in terrible pain; relationships sour; there's the loss of career or jobs; moves feel like losses too; and then, in your fifties, friends begin to die with a disturbingly annual regularity. But like that tree, I try to keep growing and sprouting leaves each spring.

It's this desire to keep growing I see in Saint Francis. And I believe he shows us how to lean into life. He too experienced failure, a forever split with a parent, a friend's betrayal, physical suffering, moments of humiliation, and death. But he was able to live his life with a flourish. Spirit seems to have filled him with hope and love in ways that make me look and say, I'd like some of that, please.

So brief investigations into his way of life to learn for myself, to share with you, are the approach I take in this book. You might even consider each of the chapters a kind of experiment in Francis living.

—

People call him a poet and artist. He was. People call him simple and naive, and he probably was those things too. Children used to throw dirt and mock him, finding him ridiculous compared to their parents and other adults living within the margins. What is most interesting to me is that if he were alive today, doing what he did then, we would likely also dismiss him. We may not throw rocks—medieval children were transparent in ways that we rarely allow ourselves to be—but we'd find him irrelevant, a fool. Or his way of living would go unnoticed. If we even noticed him, we would hold him in dismissive disdain. His actions were inexplicable, like the guy in the alley who bangs on my trash cans. Francis's teachings seem overly simple, without much to engage my desire to debate.

Yet people did notice him. People were drawn to his way of living from the start, and his movement grew like no spiritual movement had before him.

But he wasn't easy. From the distance of history, it's easy to love him today. Close up, however, he was sometimes difficult to be around. Imagine an athlete in a team sport who demands of fans in the bleachers what he demands of himself. Francis did that. Then when he was gone from the scene, on a mission or long journey, many came to join what he'd started, inspired by the stories of Francis, but they didn't know him personally. They had difficulty imagining how their famous founder could combine joy and pleasure with such severity of commitment. One or the other had to be sacrificed, they imagined. This is when some began to frame Francis in ways that failed to appreciate his art.

"While he was still living in this miserable and mournful world our blessed father Francis . . ." begins a chapter in one of the primary source materials on Francis.[1] But Francis would never have spoken of the world as miserable or mournful. And for his followers to do so was like surrounding a lush landscape painting with a sad, dull metal frame. This was in fact the frame that often surrounded his story and teachings centuries after his death.

It's only since the early 1900s that the perception of him has changed, making him the world's most popular saint. At the turn of the previous century, a renaissance of interest in Francis began, spurred on by a few people who began to tell the story of who he really was; they had to go beyond the hagiography and find the real person. The first to reveal the real Francis was Paul Sabatier, a French Protestant pastor, who published the first modern biography in 1894. It was quickly translated into a dozen other languages. Then came a Danish writer, Johannes Jorgensen, later nominated for the Nobel Prize in Literature, with another important biography. They both presented Francis as a person of contemporary relevance.

Meanwhile, a medieval folktale inspired by Francis and his holy foolery, called *The Juggler of Notre Dame*, saw the light as a magazine story, an opera, a choreographed dance, and a tale in popular children's books.

A generation later came the best film ever made about a saint: Roberto Rossellini's *The Flowers of St. Francis* in 1950, cowritten by a young Federico Fellini. All the actors, except one, were nonactors—most of them were Franciscan friars drawn to the project for personal and religious reasons. The one who played the part of Francis was not even mentioned in the credits. It was as if an "actor" couldn't portray Francis on the screen—he was too real for that. That film became one of the great classics of Italian neorealism.

Then Nikos Kazantzakis, the charismatic and controversial Greek writer who also wrote *The Last Temptation of Christ*, penned the powerful and picturesque

God's Pauper (published as *Saint Francis* in the United States), bringing the saint to life as the human he was in ways that only a novel can. In one scene describing the stigmata, for example—when Francis is purported to have received wounds matching those of Christ in his Passion, an event about which most biographers remain mostly silent for lack of evidence—Kazantzakis depicts the scene in a field on fire, with lightning flashing and Francesco yelling, "I want more!"

But before this renaissance got underway, there were those who saw Francis as an example of how the church often turns a good Christian into an irrelevant saint. Before the rediscovery of the true Francis began a little more than a century ago, he was stuck in the saccharine sweetness of cuddly animal stories. He was so saintly as to be safe for everyone but sinners and the suffering. There was no way the real Francis could be found. With his reputation locked up safely in unrelatable legends, there was little chance for his relevance and inspiring action today.

The Protestant reformer Martin Luther was among Francis's prominent critics. By the time Luther was a young monk, around 1500, Franciscans—those followers of Francis—so identified with their founder that he eclipsed reverence for Christ. Early followers of Francis were so eager to provide reasons for that level of honor that they even claimed to find Francis foretold in the Old Testament and by Christ himself.[2] A lot of what Luther protested was this kind of ridiculous leader worship, which is why Luther found such a ready audience for his critiques. No one, he said, should turn saints into idols.

This is not my approach. My hope is to see a continued renaissance of interest in Francis—the *real* Francis. This Francis was earthy and rough like burlap, not bronzed and sculpted like the baroque fountain cherubim some have made him out to be.

I've written other books about him, and I imagine some readers may wonder, *Why another?* I continue to ask myself the same question. And the answer comes back: we need accessible entrées to spiritual practice for who we are and how we live in the present moment, and Francis still offers the best set of practices I have found anywhere. So I'm setting out to make those practices simple and clear for you and me. I hope you can use this book the way someone might follow a map to a hidden treasure: once you've made it there, you have no more need of the map. Toss it away, but keep the treasure you find.

—

One afternoon recently I was talking with a group of high school students. Their teacher asked if I would introduce them to Francis of Assisi. I started out with a bit of biography and something about the times in which he lived, imagining that the medieval history would be fascinating to some. But by this time, I saw the lack of fascination on their bored faces. So I pivoted.

"OK, enough history and background. Let's try this instead. Look, for a moment, at your hands," I said.

They paused, most of them looking up suddenly at me instead. *Huh?*

"I'm serious. Do me this favor. Look at your hands. Go ahead." And then I paused for a slightly awkward length of time, as my boss taught me to do when I was sixteen and selling shoes in his store. ("Ask if they'd like to buy them and wear them home. Then remember to *wait* for the answer. Don't let them off the hook by not waiting for an answer. There may be an awkward pause.")

Most of them started to look at their hands.

"Keep your eyes there," I continued. "In fact, take your time now. Look at your fingertips. Your palms. Picture in your mind what they have recently touched or carried. What did they hold—perhaps this morning before you arrived here? What have they recently given away?"

Maybe they thought I was a bit nuts. But I persisted.

"Those hands of yours can be used to hurt, or they can be used to heal and help," I went on. "What do you use your hands for? Are you gentle with them? Did anyone teach you to be gentle with your hands?"

I began to imagine that they were grateful not to be hearing anything more about the liturgical practices of the late medieval church, the machinations of the Crusades, and Pope Innocent III, to whom Francis first appealed for permission for his religious reform movement.

I said, "OK. Let's move on. How about your mouth?

"You can't really look at your own mouth, so turn and look at the mouth of the person sitting next to you. The lips curve. They frown. They grin. Maybe they even snarl." They liked this. There was laughter as everyone seemed to choose one of these expressions.

"Now consider your own mouth. What does it most often do? Does it laugh? Kiss? Is it honest? Do you use your mouth to speak in ways that are kind?

Maybe not always? I think it is possible to throw words at people the way that we throw things, being careless or causing damage. We should be kind with our mouths."

Now they were listening carefully, which surprised me.

"Think now about your feet. Think about your feet as you look out the window at people on the street. Do you see someone in need of kindness? It is often easy to find someone who appears lonely. Do your feet move you in their direction? We often move around so quickly that we fail to notice when someone needs our help. Or, let's be honest, we don't much care. We see a need and instead we put our feet up.

"Put your heart in your feet. When was the last time you went looking for the person who needs a friend? Be honest—when was it? Whether in a classroom, at work, or on the street, it has never been easy to do the right thing because it takes a special kind of courage. We will always feel more comfortable *not* helping, avoiding new and uncomfortable situations. But we need to do more than be comfortable.

"God knows that my feet have not moved toward helping others, plenty. I'm trying today to be more courageous than I was when I was your age. I hope you'll do better than I did."

I knew, in a way, that I was preaching to the choir. These students were part of a group that I already knew felt marginalized. They were members of an LGBTQ club on campus. Then I added, "In all of this, I have to tell you, I am channeling the teachings of the medieval saint I was talking about before. He's been immortalized in birdbaths everywhere, which is unfortunate. You see, this is how Francis of Assisi imagined his role in the world: in very practical ways, using his hands, his mouth, and his feet."

Thomas Aquinas, another medieval saint, used to say that beauty is whatever gives pleasure on sight. He said that identifying beauty came from an intuitive understanding that people might cultivate. He said this after Gothic cathedrals had been built. He admired craftwork, fine art, flourishes of brushes and chisels and carvings, which could be found in churches all over Europe.

But Francis never said a word about beauty. Unlike Thomas, Francis was an artist—a poet, a musician, and a dancer. Thomas worked only in words. Having studied Francis's life for twenty-five years now, I'll tell you the single most interesting thing about him is that he shows what he believes rather than tells it. He didn't indicate that he cared a whit about lovely buildings and whatever the best new carvings were.

The artist Francis found his inspiration in people and other creatures, who they are and what they do in the world around him, as well as in the heavens.

He shows ways of following Jesus that involve the most ordinary and tangible expressions of how to live. He wasn't about theological flights of fancy or religious arguments. He actually begged his spiritual brothers and sisters *not* to study theology or immerse themselves in books, so worried was he that study and reading would function like a bucket of cold water on the hot coals of their original passions. So why another book?

Because Francis remained focused on being gentle, paying attention, listening and companionship, embracing the uncomfortable (even inside himself), looking for the vulnerable, and not being afraid. These are some of the things that I am trying to do in this book. And when these insights from the real Francis move into your heart, feet, mouth, and hands, then this book, this map, can be put down.

Chapter 1

FIND YOUR SIBLINGS

He started out as Giovanni, "John," with the surname Bernardone, born to privilege. His father was away on business at the time, so his mother, Pica, named him. We unfortunately know almost nothing else about her. And when Pietro returned to find he had a son, he renamed him after the place he loved most: "Francesco," for France. *Francis*.

Pietro was so successful in business that he traveled abroad to source and sell his wares: silks and fancy clothes. Most people then were bound tightly to their places. Roads were for knights going to fight, royal messengers moving between royal courts, and the occasional prelate on a mission, with soldier-attendants along for safety. And for people like Pietro.

Francis probably accompanied him on some of his trips. Imagine a cart piled high with silks—purples, scarlets, deep blacks—pulled by donkeys and guided by servants along dusty Roman roads. Father and son rode high on their horses, moving from Umbria through Tuscany and Florence, around the sea to Genova, or north over Alpine passes, toward open and free markets, aided by local guides who were paid for the information and security they provided. This was in about the year 1195. One of those markets, in the Champagne region of France, is where Pietro and his son probably met traders from all over the world.

About fourteen years later when he was founding a new religious order, circa 1209, Francis wrote in his *Rule*, a document spelling out precepts of what their life was to be about, "I command all of the brothers . . . when they travel about the world, or reside in various places, that they never have animals with them, or entrust an animal to the care of others, or in any other way keep one. They should also never ride on horseback unless they absolutely must do so for reasons of sickness or some other great necessity."[1]

Why would a young man leave the horses and the market and the adventures of mercantile behind? Francis began to question the comfort and wisdom his father provided. How strange it must have seemed to Francis's highborn friends, and to his father, when he did. Francis loved horses. He loved fine things. At some point between trips, Pietro outfitted his son in fine armor, sending him off to crusade in the company of other men trying to make names for themselves. If Francis didn't want to be a silk trades- man, that was OK; he could be a knight instead. But fighting didn't go well for him, and he came back in disgrace.

With Pietro angry and humiliated, Francis began to not only question his position in the world but dis- dain it. He began to see beyond his privilege, though he also loved his friends and partied with them. He was well liked and easygoing, and he always had money.

But soon after that failed crusading, he began walking alone in the woods and visiting caves in the mountains. He began conversing with God. His friends, confused, watched their carefree Francis turn into . . . something else almost overnight.

Has he caught a fever?

Perhaps it's his father who is demanding more of his time.

But no, there he is again, not with Bernardone . . . but leaving the city gates, walking up into the hills.

He began to steal from his father, selling those fancy silks to give money to the poor. For the first time, he was realizing that there were people in need, even living close by, and that he had a responsibility to help them. With the impulse of a teenager, he often acted poorly; he was self-righteous, justifying stealing from his father. He considered himself a sort of Robin Hood, giving the money to the poor.

Then the situation got worse.

One late fall afternoon, the whole town was gathered in front of the bishop's palace to witness a confrontation between Pietro and his now wayward, confused son. The crowd grew, and some climbed trees for a better view of the scene. The Umbrian sun was cold, casting long shadows on the stone piazza. The bishop was awkward. He didn't want trouble. The only one looking for trouble that day was Pietro, who demanded respect. In front of the bishop and the town, he laid out his case, refusing to look at Francis as he did, directing himself to the prelate who he believed could exact an apology and the necessary obedience from his son.

Francis listened, looking around at the hundreds of faces staring back at him, people he'd known his whole life. What he must have been thinking at that moment, I wish I knew. Most people who experience defeat, embarrassment, and family discord and who so radically change who they are leave their childhood friends behind before it all plays out in front of them. Not Francis. Everyone he knew must have been looking on at that moment. I can't imagine the intense gaze that the crowd must have placed upon Francis.

In an act of defiance, he stripped naked. As if to make real what had already been done to him metaphorically, in front of everyone, including his father and the bishop and the people hanging from the trees, Francis removed every single thing. Thomas of Celano, the first Francis biographer, says that he took everything off and threw them on the ground. Another account says that he paused and folded them. What a spectacle: a public referendum at first on Francis, then turning the gaze, the judgment, on his father. The scene would have elicited a mixture of laughter and gasps from those who watched as Francis stripped the remnants of his father's influence from himself and laid them at his father's feet. Respect?

"I only have a father in heaven now," he said, with what would become a characteristic flair. The bishop, in the middle of this embarrassing scene, grabbed a cassock and quickly draped it over Francis's narrow shoulders. He must have then shrugged to Pietro. There was no stopping the fearlessness of this young man.

Francis may have lacked courage wearing a knight's armor, but he seemed valiant wearing nothing at all. He had found something else, something brighter and bolder that allowed him to be free.

Many other well-known saints have anecdotes of their childhood, their birth, and even their conception to demonstrate how they were prepared for holiness, as if what they did in their adult lives was a foregone conclusion, evidence of sanctity, explained with miracles. Of Francis, there are no such stories.

In fact, we can assume that rather than a life formed in a string of supernatural events, Francis was lonely as a child. We know that he had siblings, but nothing in his teachings or stories or accounts speaks of them.

Instead, the witness of Francis's life is that families of origin can be . . . very messy. When he took off his clothes, he ended up rejecting his father. He didn't choose his siblings.

What he did next was leave the town for the dark silence of those caves in the mountains before heading for the way of the open road. As G. K. Chesterton memorably describes the moment, "He went out half-naked . . . a man without a father. He was penniless, he was parentless, he was to all appearances without a trade or a plan or a hope in the world, and as he went under the frosty trees, he burst suddenly into song."[2]

Francis wasn't drawn to the security of a monastery. He sought God alone. Security, he wanted to let go of. In those days, in the early 1200s, monastery life provided an alternative parentage suitable for a misfit like Francis. In a monastery, he would have elders who could answer his questions and guide him in sure ways. He would have the certainty of food on the table, a fine education, structure and order for his days, books for learning, and a choir or craft to busy his mind and hands. He could have channeled his desire for seeking God and virtue behind a monastery's thick stone walls.

But Francis was drawn elsewhere, to places undefined. Strangely, he wanted a spiritual life that was unpredictable, without guarantees, without abbots, without securities. How unusual this was, and still is. He'd heard the Gospels (*heard* them; he likely didn't read), and he knew that what Jesus wanted from human beings was much simpler—and more beautiful, more human—than anything he'd ever heard in church.

Given this, it is amazing that Francis of Assisi didn't go down in history as a heretic but instead became the world's most appreciable saint. He went on to create a life and body of teachings that still astound people centuries later. He said we are responsible for ourselves and for each other. We are to be gentle, to love dangerously, and not to care about what may happen tomorrow. He made his life an embodiment of the Beatitudes in Jesus's Sermon on the Mount, which praises the peacemaker and honors the poor.

The responsibility we have for ourselves and each other is given to us before belief, before birth or baptism; it's given in creation. Everyone born is made in God's image, and for everyone born there's the opportunity to live the creative, inspired life of God's Holy Spirit. This divine spirit didn't require a recitation of a creed, a belief in dogma or baptism (though Francis was sure baptism helped). The spirit of God inhabits existence, being. God has been "eternally pregnant" with creation, as Meister Eckhart said, and "human beings should know and understand how noble being is."[3] Francis had a similar sense of the nobility of creation, as evidenced in his magnificent song "The Canticle of the Creatures," the oldest known poem in the Italian vernacular, which we'll delve into deeply in a later chapter.

Each of his writings—whether canticle, letter, or rule—brought out an understanding of this very sense of life and being and spirit. But the most controversial sentence Francis ever wrote was in his "Testament"—a sort of last will, what we call today a "spiritual testament." Halfway through a simple seven-hundred-word document, he says, "No one showed me what I was supposed to do, but the Most High revealed to me that I should live according to the ways of the Gospel."

What happened to the one Holy Catholic Church of his creed? What happened to his parish priest, his bishop? Where are the sacraments of the church? Those things were still there, and Francis was faithful to them to the end, but he also acknowledged the primary vitality of a direct relationship with God.

There was nothing more important—before, after, or during his life—than that. He was simply being truthful about and honest to his experience.

Wait. That isn't precisely what he wrote. I left out one important word. I also left out the short sentence that precedes that sentence. Here is the fuller version, with the missing parts in bold: "**Then God gave me brothers**. No one **else** showed me what I was supposed to do, but the Most High revealed to me that I should live according to the ways of the Gospel."

Francis was given God *and* community (his spiritual siblings, his housemates, his neighbors, his friends and colleagues, his moral and religious family, every human being . . .), and he vowed to be faithful, listening to them, as to what he should do next. No path was certain, but some were better worn than others.

All of us, I think, might understand that this is what we need. In choosing God and choosing those who are brothers, sisters, siblings, or kin to us, we show how none of us are expected to walk alone.

Chapter 2

FEED THE WOLF

You have to see the black-and-white photographs of Mahatma Gandhi stepping out of a car (they insisted on driving him) wearing cassock and sandals, having come to London to meet with the king of England, in order to grasp what it must have looked like to see Francis anywhere near the halls of power of his day. The little friar must have looked similarly out of place and outside of time whenever he was required to visit a bishop, lord, or pope.

Much more often, Francis was visiting with ordinary creatures, and one of those he called "Brother Wolf."

There have always been wolves that frighten us, and some of them have taken on legendary, mythical proportions. Since ancient days, there have been stories of wild animals that, for whatever reason (maybe disease or a harsh winter), attack human beings and "develop a taste for human flesh." I don't know if that actually has happened, but don't tell a villager from one of the hamlets where these stories originated that it is false. Wild dogs were feared with a terror that often turned to paranoia. Simply the mention of a threatening sighting could set a hunting team on horseback into the woods, carrying spears and accompanied by a pack of hunting dogs.

The most notable legendary beast preyed on the people of Gevaudan in the Languedoc of France, terrorizing them for several years in the second half of the eighteenth century. In some tellings, the beast was a werewolf. Others said a giant hyena. Some naturalists have wondered if it might have been a mountain lion. Certain theologians called it a devilish scourge. More likely, it was a small pack of large wolves. One day, one of them was killed and presented to King Louis XV in Versailles, so infamous was its crimes, and all of France breathed a sigh of relief. Until another throat was ripped out. This beast or beasts killed children at play and women walking home from errands, and almost always the throat was ripped from the body. Mobs of citizens were formed to hunt it down.

Five hundred years earlier, another creature was stalking farm animals and attacking the citizens of the town of Gubbio in Umbria. The people of Gubbio asked Francis of Assisi to help rid them of the fearsome beast who threatened the town's inhabitants. When he arrived at the scene, the first thing that Francis did surprised everyone. He went out into the town to meet the wolf. What those who watched from the cracks in their doors and windows witnessed was this: For the first few minutes, the wolf began to size up the little friar like prey. But then, the two began to talk. (As we have come to see, and I don't mean this in any way cynically, the saint was able to communicate with all sorts of creatures.) Francis quickly discerned that, above all, the wolf was hungry.

The Gubbians watching the scene were dumbfounded.

What's he doing?

Did you explain to him that we don't want the wolf to remain?

A hedgehog is unwelcome here, let alone wolves that want to eat us.

Who is this friar?

Someone said they've heard of him.

A boy from Assisi who preaches on street corners?

He's the person we called for?

This is a dragon we're dealing with!

Our weapons have been useless against it!

We need a knight with a lance, not a mendicant with a begging bowl.

After the scene unfolded in front of them, Francis turned to the townspeople with a request and brokered a deal between them and the creature. He arranged for the one whom he now called Brother Wolf and the people to care for each other. As the town and the wolf settled into the agreement, the people came to see their new sibling, Brother Wolf, as one among them who needed easy and regular access to life's necessities.

This is not the first episode in Francis's life of conversion—a life of changing toward God and for others—but it is the culmination. This is also a scene from his life that brings home a lesson for every follower of Jesus everywhere: your growth, maturation, spiritual conversion is not for yourself, but for the community.

Francis certainly understood conversion that way. In the opening paragraph of his "Testament"—one of his last writings, which is largely autobiographical—he frames his conversion as foregoing worldly things for the purpose of working for mercy: "The Lord gave me, Brother Francis, the ability to do penance in the following way: When I was in sin, even the sight of lepers was like acid to me. But the Lord himself led me among them, and I worked mercy with them, and helped them. When I left, all that had been so acidic to me was turned into sweetness in my soul and my body. And shortly afterward, I got up and left the world."[1] That feeling of "sweetness in my soul and my body"—where could it come from, if not from moments in his life such as going out to meet the Wolf of Gubbio and feeding him?

These are the questions the agreement of Gubbio unveils for us:

Why do we feed the wolf? *We feed the wolf because he's hungry.*

And why is he hungry? *We should find out. Every wolf has a story.*

We pass wolves on the street every day. We are all, at times, wolves ourselves.

—

I was recently talking with a friend who works in the district attorney's office where I live who has participated in court-appointed restorative justice sessions between prostitutes and the johns who hire them. At one of these sessions, she told me, one man listened to the woman across the table speak of childhood trauma and abuse that she had suffered. It was in this context that she found herself beginning to turn tricks, she explained in painful detail.

Listening to her words, the man looked at her and said, so that everyone in the room that day could hear, "I honestly didn't, until just now, see you as a human being." He seemed shocked to hear himself saying these words; he knew how terrible it sounded. It wasn't a performance for leniency, my friend explained, because the man's sentence had already been served.

We often don't respect members of our own species as one of us—let alone the other animals who cross our path. But every wolf has a story, including the wolf who refused to see the fellow human as a person. Including the wolf who judges but does not see the creature in front of them.

It is astonishing by any measure, medieval or twenty-first century, how Francis went out to meet the Wolf of Gubbio. Presented with a situation he didn't understand and a creature he probably had never encountered, that was his first gesture: to meet it. The original tale says, "A fearsome wolf, made crazy with severe hunger, was devouring both animals and human beings. The people of Gubbio were terrified and took to carrying weapons with them wherever they went. But even weapons did not keep them safe from this wolf. Before long, they stopped going outside the city gates altogether. But God wanted Francis to show the people of Gubbio a better way."

I was recently reading an essay by the nature writer Edward Hoagland, who wrote of how mountain lions "spirit themselves away in saw-toothed canyons and . . . when conversing with their mates they coo like pigeons, sob like women, emit a flat slight shriek, a popping bubbling growl, or mew, or yowl. . . . They ramble as much as twenty-five miles in a night. . . . It's a solitary, busy life."[2] Wolves are similar.

In *The Wisdom of Wolves*, Jim and Jamie Dutcher, experts on wolf behavior, write, "Wolves can be described in many ways, but above all they are social.

They need each other. As hunters, as parents, as keepers of a home territory, wolves succeed as part of a group." Later they add what six years of observing a particular pack of wolves in the Idaho wilderness has taught them: "Like many other animals, they are emotionally intelligent beings. A wolf knows who he is, and he sees his packmates as individuals. He has a concept of how his actions are perceived by others. He is capable of empathy, compassion, apology, and encouragement."[3]

Soon after the Wolf of Gubbio, there was an actual dog saint in France. Saint Guinefort was a greyhound from the later part of that century who, according to legend, killed a snake in order to save a child and as a result achieved local veneration. But this is how we oversweeten a story, turning it into something it wasn't. Brother Wolf wasn't a saint. He was simply a hungry and damaged creature in need.

Peter Maurin, cofounder with Dorothy Day of the Catholic Worker movement, once said, "While modern society calls beggars bums and panhandlers, they are in fact the Ambassadors of God."

There's a tradition in Judaism that says that you are to care for any strangers who present themselves, no matter who they are, where you are, or what circumstances might suggest you do instead, because a stranger could for all you know be the Messiah, and if you don't care for them, the Messiah's return may be thwarted.

Another tradition in Judaism, even more common, suggests that, like the Hebrew prophets in the Scriptures, there isn't so much one single messiah as there are people of God who can bring to pass a messianic age. Prayerfully waiting for someone to come is replaced by working to bring about a time when even wolves won't go hungry. This is the clearest Christian understanding of responsibility too.

Even evolutionary biology and physics tell us this. At least intellectually, we realize now, better than any generation before us, how one life impacts another and how living our lives is completely reliant upon the lives of every other creature and all of the lives that have come before us. We do not, and cannot, live alone—in any sense of that word. Perhaps our common understanding of other species in the past was to dominate them mostly because we were unable to grasp our interconnectedness.

One of the suggested interpretations about the Wolf of Gubbio is that the rampaging beast was not in fact a wolf but a human being. In Italian, the word for wolf, *lupo*, can also sometimes be a man's name, and in the region surrounding Gubbio at this time, there was a certain Friar Lupo who had met Francis and undergone a conversion sometime after committing a terrible crime of violence. Some sources tell us that Francis and Friar Lupo traveled together to Spain in later years. But that's all we know of this Lupo.

If the wolf was a human being, would that change the meaning of what happened in Gubbio? Not much, but I understand the motivation to disenchant the tale. The stories of Francis and animals can at times become silly: when fish come to the surface of a lake to bow to him, or when wild animals eat from his hand, we have good reason to think about putting the legends away and moving on to something more relevant. Even the original telling of the Wolf of Gubbio adds, when Francis is talking with the creature, "The wolf moved its tail and ears and nodded its head." OK.

Other saints have animal stories too, and they often teeter toward the quaint. There's the Celtic Saint Kevin, for instance, who was so holy that he held a blackbird in his outstretched hands until the bird laid and hatched its eggs. OK.

Wolves appear throughout our fairy tales, along with virtuous queens, dangerous sirens, and abandoned children. Think of "Little Red Riding Hood," "The Boy Who Cried Wolf," and "The Three Little

Pigs." At the center of all these stories is the image of the Big Bad Wolf, first found in Aesop's fables six hundred years before Christ, and used as a standard since then in the folklore of every country wolves inhabit. The frightening, menacing predator. Big teeth and slobber. Darkness over light. All of the archetypes—or prejudices—of our worst dreams.

Folklorists and anthropologists tell us that these fables and fairy tales probably had their origin in real threats. Wolves really *did* sometimes threaten communities and devour travelers in dark woods centuries ago. And child psychologists remind us that we create stories about what frightens us in order to come to terms with those frights.

The Wolf of Gubbio is different from all of these others—both the fairy tales and the saintly silly stories. This particular wolf seems human. Those wolves of Aesop's might as well be dragons. And if he's not human, Brother Wolf's needs are precisely those of human beings everywhere—even his solitariness, followed by his desire for community.

Today, Francis's approach to hunger and fear, and his respect and partnering with Brother Wolf, makes sense to us. Most of all because we recognize that there are still plenty of wolves—and every wolf needs to eat. Plain and simple. Why leave them hungry and live afraid? There's a reason wolves get hungry, remain hungry, and become threatening. Why is it that we often don't believe it's our job to meet them, understand them, feed them? When we overcome our fears and do what's right, we meet the wolf, sometimes in ourselves, and begin to understand that we are all wolves, after all, at one time or another.

Chapter 3

PUT YOUR WEAPONS DOWN

You'll notice that this book is unlike the many others that suggest the world pivoted on Francis's influence. We've had enough of the "Great Man of History" view of things, and it was never an accurate approach. The world doesn't orbit around any one person, and as we painfully discover over and over again, no "great" person is as great as we (or they) sometimes imagine.

To Francis, it would be contrary to the spirit he lived by to suggest that he was a person of significant influence and power. He was precisely the opposite. He was weak and vulnerable. And that was his path.

As I mentioned in chapter 1, as a young man, he went off to war, seeking fame, caught up in the crusading spirit. But there is more to that story. Francis was captured as a prisoner, and it was his father who bailed him out. The next time—because he often made the same mistake twice—Francis joined other soldiers dressed up in the best protective armor, with the finest weaponry his father could afford. But he soon returned to Assisi utterly defeated. He was either ill or deserted or both; the sources differ. In Assisi, he then laid down his weapons for good, realizing that they could do nothing for him, offer him nothing.

It was soon after these experiences that Francis turned to religious and spiritual life. When he did so, he again sought no "religious" armor or weapons.

He knew early on that he didn't want to be a monk. That would have been the obvious path to take, but he didn't want the set-apart-ness of Benedictine monastic life at that time. Tall stone walls were a fortress that kept the world at bay for those who were lucky or had wealthy enough parents to send their sons to a monastery in the country. There was no aspect of western European culture that was better defined and more orderly than monasticism. Performing the liturgy with precision around the clock was most of all how monasteries "sought to control the future."[1] A clockwork liturgical existence helped explain life, conveying order in a world that, outside their walls, could quickly feel dangerous, fleeting, and random.

No, Francis didn't see himself behind such walls, quietly working and praying his days away, not that he saw anything wrong with that for others.

But how his mother must have wanted at least that measure of security for her son who was leaving behind all that was the protective armor of his old life!

Your father shows no respect for monks, I know, but he recognizes their influence. More than once, I have seen him negotiate with an abbot.

A religious life is not what we had ever imagined for you, my talented son, but at least in the monastery you would be safe.

You will have books.

You will have friends.

You will have the safety of the church.

Francis avoided the priesthood too. In both sincerity and savvy, his instincts all pointed toward ordinary sanctity and responsibility as the vocation of every human being. He held a discomfort with status and pride, which the priesthood easily fed into. Most of all, one didn't need a collar to do what he felt called to do.

James Cowan, a writer best known for championing aboriginal lives and teachings, makes this remark in his little book on Francis, describing the arc of Francis's path of conversion: "He had not yet attained to that inwardness of spirit that would enable him to make a fundamental decision about himself: that he had no choice but to lead the life of a homeless ascetic, a celestial wanderer. What lay ahead for him was not the cloistered life of a monk, or the privileged preserve of a bishop, but that of a perpetual outsider."[2]

While he would always love and reverence Christ in the holy sacrament and the priestly vocation that blesses it, Francis didn't hesitate to say that he and his humble, uneducated friars should preach in the streets—even as he always politely asked permission of the local priest or bishop to do so. Among the stories about him are absent the disrespectful anecdotes such as the one about an earlier Italian saint, Ranieri: "Before Ranieri cures the epileptic priest who has sought out the layman's miraculous cures, the saint asked the priest whether or not he believed that God had sent him to bring about this cure. . . . Ranieri only healed the priest once such an assurance has been given."[3] Francis's approach to these matters—taking out the power dynamic—as savvy as it was in respectful requests, is one reason we've all heard about Francis and almost none of us have heard of Ranieri.

As his path became clear after visiting the caves, he set out on his chosen ministry to gather stones and repair fallen churches. And he seems to have lived and slept vulnerably as a homeless person would, during that time, in ruins without roofs, in open spaces. He then began to serve lepers he met who often lived outside of towns and cities, as homeless as himself. He was determined to touch them and live among them, something that became central to his purpose.[4] At first, they frightened him. Visually, they repulsed him. He wasn't proud of that, but it was true. When the body is affected by leprosy, the soft tissue begins to waste away. The bones of the hands, feet, and face are also frequently infected, resulting in the loss of digits (fingers, toes) and joints (jawbone).

He wasn't alone in feeling repulsed and frightened. Everyone at that time responded to the disease with fear. Local priests even devised ceremonies through which to bless those afflicted while still forbidding them to mingle with the unafflicted. "I forbid you to enter church, monastery, fair, mill, marketplace or tavern," they would recite. "I forbid you ever to leave your house without your leper's costume . . . to touch a well, or well cord, without your gloves . . . to eat or drink, except with lepers."[5]

Bonaventure's *Major Legend* of Francis says, "He moved to the lepers and stayed with them," adding with extraordinary detail, "He washed their feet, bound up their sores, drew the pus from their wounds and wiped away the discharge, kissing their wounds with a miraculous devotion."[6]

Soon people began to want to join him in his work. Francis told them that there was a prerequisite to joining his band of friars: giving away all their possessions. But very quickly, then, he added that they must take turns serving lepers in the ways that he was learning to do. It was no longer acceptable to live apart from the sick and unpleasant. One of the early Franciscans remarked that Francis had a "joyful and genuine love of humble and rejected persons."[7] Personal vulnerability was required, putting one's weapons—of privilege, authority, status, stature—down.

Anyone who works among people on the streets knows that some are there because they're escaping an abusive relationship. It can feel safer to be on the streets than to be at home where you may be beaten up, raped, or killed. Some pious chroniclers of the late Middle Ages used to compare Francis of Assisi to Christ, showing their close similarity. They would say that Francis was beaten like Christ—that his father beat him, robbers beat him, children pelted him with mud and rocks, the "Saracens" (what medieval Christians called Arab Muslims) beat him when he went to meet with the sultan, and devils beat him when he was trying to pray. With the exception of the children, there's little evidence of any of this. But he came to understand those who are physically vulnerable.

Francis's father indulged him and then wanted nothing to do with him. When Francis sought peace and an end to the Crusades and pilgrimaged to meet the sultan, the sultan's men seemed bemused by him—a Christian holy man talking of love and brotherhood, surrounded by crusaders. More likely it was the crusaders who wanted to beat the crap out of the saint, for disdaining their culture of war and attempting nonviolent cooperation with a sworn enemy. As for devils, they may be the most real of all, but Francis didn't speak of them.

But most of all, it's those mocking children who return to mind as I reflect, Why did they do it? Perhaps it is simple. They had no other adult examples of laying down weapons, of refusing to threaten others in order to get what they want or deserve, of kindness bestowed on those who are essentially powerless.

When they saw Francis and his open, gentle hands, they could only laugh and throw stones. That's what we do when we're really afraid, and we're most afraid of the unfamiliar unknown. It's the unfamiliar unknown that Francis meets, like the wolf, with no weapons and seeming powerlessness.

Chapter 4

LIVE SIMPLY, EMBRACE PATCHWORK

When we met Francis in chapter 1, he removed all his clothes and, according to one account, folded them neatly (what a detail!), returning them to his father. He didn't want those fancy things anymore, and frankly, he didn't want his father around him anymore either. But Francis continued to see the relevance of clothes to his life. He knew that clothes reveal things about us, whether we like it or not.

When he began to write the rules for those following the way of life that he was creating, the first requirement was to sell everything you own and give the money to the poor. Then he asked you to assist in tending to the needs of the neediest, the lepers in town. And to mark yourself as someone now walking the way of conversion, Francis said, "give him the habit [clothes] of probation for one year." Clothes would mark the intentions. In this respect, Francis was adopting and adapting from the Rule of Benedict, which said that a monk should be dressed in a particular way. According to Francis, these clothes were specific: "Two tunics without hood, a cord, pants, and a simple chaperon reaching down to the cord."[1] A chaperon was a kind of cape or hood, for warmth in colder weather. Nothing else.

I've often wondered where his love of the poor, and for being poor, first began.

When Francis experienced humiliation early as an adult, tail between his legs, a failure in battle, he walked home after his dad bailed him out of jail. The crusading knight wasn't in him and never would be. Then when he was first living his vow of poverty, when no one yet respected him for it, he and his few fellow friars had so little success begging for bread that, as one early account says, "they were compelled to eat turnips."[2] Eating raw turnips is an act of utter desperation. I've read of homeless people and people dying of starvation alone lost in the wilderness who had only raw turnips in their stomachs.

He was also an unattractive man. Don't believe the paintings that show him otherwise; artists have preferred to visualize him in an idealized form. Francesco Bernardone was not tall, handsome, or fair; he was short and swarthy.

It is said that Francis used to sometimes beg beside a Brother Masseo, one of the young men who was early to follow him. Masseo was tall and handsome. They would stand in different spots in town, and Masseo would receive excellent gleanings on his street corners while Francis was given only the smallest, crudest of things. This is reported in early accounts almost as if it were a social science experiment.

The legends of the saint obscure these scenes. It's not Francis's wonders but his failures and embarrassments that make him able to speak most poignantly, meaningfully, and relevantly to us. Too many saints levitate, bilocate, and leap tall mountains in a single bound, but fewer have obviously unachieved goals, complete disappointments, and friends who abandon them at critical moments—as Francis did.

Who is this man, that people should follow him?

He is a failure, a fool, a grown man who is still acting like a child, refusing all responsibility.

This is not what men of religion do.

These failures became for Francis moments for working on an inner life. Times of turning from the outward to the inward, from noise to quiet, from self-consumed to self-contained, can be when we discover God. He surely never read Augustine's *Confessions*, but if he had, he'd have resonated with that memorable line of honesty about the philosopher's early years when Augustine exclaims (in an *Oh my God* sort of way): "You were within me, but I was outside myself."[3]

In his new clothes, designed to be unimportant, Francis began to be quiet and spend long times in prayer. It is as if he could finally disappear. This is what led him to figure out who he was. Gandhi once said, "Prayer has been the saving of my life. Without it I should have been a lunatic long ago."[4]

The new clothes were designed to go unnoticed. There wasn't a prescribed color—in fact, the color wasn't supposed to matter. What mattered was that the fabric should be humble and earthy, fabric descriptions that Francis preferred to the effects of his father's foreign dyes and silks. Soon he would praise the patching of clothes, asking every friar to do this as necessary. In the earliest rules of the order, he said, "The brothers should always be clothed in poor, simple garments, and they may then mend them, lovingly patching them with sackcloth and other pieces, for the Lord says in the Gospel: 'Someone dressed in soft robes? Look, those who put on fine clothing and live in luxury are in royal palaces.' Even if they [the friars] are called hypocrites, let them never stop doing good and let them never desire rich clothes in this world, so that instead they may have a garment in the kingdom of heaven." He was—quite seriously—one of the earliest adopters of renew and reuse.

This simple way of life was soon extended to members of the Third Order—those in the way of Francis who do not leave their responsibilities of family and work in the world but who take vows to follow the way of Francis where they are. Francis said to them, "As to clothing, anyone who seeks to belong to this siblinghood should dress humbly."[5]

With such deliberate humility—strange in religious people of any era—come other bits of strangeness and freedom.

When he began to forget about his clothes, Francis was able to become a holy fool. If he was feeling unprepared or unwell, he talked about these feelings, willing to share his vulnerabilities with the people around him. I love this about him, and I want to be courageous enough to do the same. What it must feel like to allow oneself not to care about the judgments of others, to be happy, filled with God's happiness.

Francis's foolishness began when he removed the clothes that covered up who he really was. He tossed them to the feet of his father, who had purchased them all, as if to say, *I don't want to hide anymore.* He didn't then run off to a nudist colony. He found other clothes, humble clothes, to replace the fake ones his father had picked out for him.

Dancers talk about feeling the heat in another body as they dance. They talk about listening for the other person's body, not just watching for it. There is an intimacy to the way that they hold hands, embrace, and look into the face of another dancer. That is unlike most of the rest of us—or at least it's unlike me. Francis was that kind of dancer, and I think he came to see that his concern for what he wore was standing in the way of dancing with others.

Throwing off the silks also became a way of freedom toward the outside world of creation. One doesn't climb trees or spend afternoons in caves dressed finely. "In nature nothing exists alone," says Rachel Carson in *Silent Spring*.

And that sense of oneness exponentially increased. The Scottish writer Robert Louis Stevenson, when young, once went canoeing with a friend and slept under the stars. The whole trip made him so happy that he said he thought he understood what Buddhists speak of as Nirvana. "It may be best figured by supposing yourself to get dead drunk, and yet keep sober to enjoy it," Stevenson said. There was freedom in stripping off the clothes.

He was also way ahead of his time when it came to intuiting the potential harm in what other people took for granted. In one of my earliest books about Francis, I wrote about Francis's dislike of owning devotional books, which seems counterintuitive for a religious leader to teach his followers; perhaps it had to do with him being uncomfortable with the animals that were killed at that time to make books.[6] But now I also think that the saint's desire for drab, inexpensive, and colorless clothes had something to do with his understanding of the possible negative effects of dyes, international rather than local commerce, wealth accumulation, where dyes often were costly and imported, and those who worked in mines, harvest fields, and minerals were not paid fair wages. Even having dyed clothing could be a source of pride for someone wearing deep blacks and vibrant purples.

Most of all, fancy clothes masked Francis from the world, like a court performer or a street musician who wears a mask to play a part. There was one other incident, before his conversion, when he was still in those fancy silks of his father's, that is important to understanding this perspective. Francis joined a pilgrimage to Rome as one pilgrim among many. He knew no one of the fellow travelers. Praying at the tomb of Saint Peter one afternoon, after throwing all of his coins between the bars that separated pilgrims from the relics, he went outside: "Just as he was leaving, passing the doors of the church, he saw many poor people there begging alms. Secretly, he arranged with one of them to exchange clothes. Then, standing on the steps of the church as one of them, he gladly begged for alms himself."[7]

So, even a couple years before that meeting with his father in front of the town, Francis had been burning inside to change his clothes for good. He no longer wanted to wear a mask. He would go on playing—performing and singing, sorrowing and laughing and dancing—but without trying to be someone else. Such vulnerability became his way of learning who he was and his role in the world.

For many of his followers and many of us, it can take years to begin to see who we really are and recognize what's keeping us from that truth. When we begin to take away the clothes, the masks, the things that hide us, we begin to see ourselves and what we've hidden behind.

I have friends who recently moved to California after living in the same Manhattan apartment for thirty years. In New York, they lived nine floors up. To look out of their windows was to see only other tall buildings, steel, glass, and sky—unless you looked down, and then the taxi cabs and pedestrians were quite small. In delightful contrast, just outside the windows of their new ground-level home in Southern California are fruit trees, dahlias and fuchsia, small hills of green grass, squirrels scampering, and birds gathering around feeders. They are enjoying the change.

In both places, they have always made it a spiritual practice to care for stray cats. They've fostered them, and they've adopted them. At times they've had a dozen cats at once in their apartment. When they moved to California, they had just three elderly ones left, but they deliberately picked a new home with a solarium that features floor-to-ceiling windows looking out on all of those beautiful things of the natural world that I mentioned.

They put the cats' food and water and their play structure in that airy, sunshine-filled room. They figured the cats, who needed to continue to remain indoors for their own safety and for the safety of other small animals and birds in the neighborhood, would spend most of their remaining days in that beautiful room, looking out those enormous windows on all the things cats find most exciting. Cat TV, you might say.

My own felines love the flies and bees that come and go on the window screen in warm weather. They follow the occasional squirrel on the patio with their eyes and those happy, twitching feet. And the birds that flitter around in the bushes and the trees. Martin and Rosa love their window sits. My friends in California, however, were surprised by what happened next.

Their cats didn't even notice. Those giant windows seemed to be nothing but walls to them. When they were sitting in front of one, they never even looked outside. Their three cats were healthy and well, but they didn't seem to be able to see what was beyond the room in which they were living. My surprised friends began to grasp why this might be. All the cats had ever known was their ninth-floor apartment in New York City, they reasoned; and since cats don't admire skyscrapers or distant airplanes, they had been conditioned to see nothing beyond their immediate four walls of existence. Their senses were stunted.

It wasn't the fault of the cats. It's not necessarily our fault; Francis knew that the things that stop us from meeting ourselves are all around, and they slowly cover for us the true story, the true green world outside, often without our noticing, and slowly over time. We no longer see what is there right in front of our eyes. It is as if we're in a solarium full of windows and there is so much to behold—but we're mostly blind to it. We don't see the world as it is; we learn to see instead what we want to see. We create our world with what we think, often unconsciously, that we need. Those are the "clothes" that Francis threw off as well when he left his father behind that day in the piazza.

Chapter 5

TOUCH WHAT'S FRIGHTENING

This is completely counterintuitive, I know that. Whatever is frightening, we usually steer clear of. We run away. We run away from falling trees, dangerous parts of town, snarling dogs, and that which we know will trigger in us an upsetting response. And if we don't run, we at least tend to leave alone the frightening thing. *Don't touch that!* Like the wasps' nest that seems to be building in the eaves above my garage.

For most of us, our everyday lives, ordinary as they are, are probably designed to avoid what's scary. I own a home, and it usually keeps out most unwanted things with sturdy walls and locked doors and windows. I own a car, and it does the same. I watch what I want to watch; I read what I want to read; I go mostly where I choose to go; I see the people whom I want to see.

Why should we do otherwise? This seems to be working fine, controlling our environments, keeping in what we want to keep in, and out what potentially might harm or disturb us.

Imagine the long journey Francis made, traveling to meet the sultan in the Nile Delta. It's never told as an example of overcoming fear and barriers, but imagine what it must have looked like to Francis and his companion.

Exhausted and thirsty when they approached by boat, they must have felt the warm, humid air of an Egyptian summer, and when they stepped foot onto the desert sands, they would have observed colorful lotus flowers, summer terns hunting for shellfish in moving tides, and towering palm trees swaying in the breeze before arriving at the sprawling human camps nearby.

Francis had arrived in Damietta, where the Mediterranean Sea meets the Nile River.

Thousands of soldiers lay there, waiting. Their leader, Pelagio Galvani, priest and canon lawyer, not soldier, was made a cardinal of the church and elected head of the Latin church in Antioch when Antioch was under Muslim control. His designated job was to lead the fight to return the region "to Christ"—that is, to Christian control. So the Fifth Crusade was on, and the region lay full of Western soldiers preparing for battle. Each had sworn to fight with religious devotion.

In that desert scene, the sultan received word that two barefoot men—Francis and his companion, Brother Illuminato—had crossed enemy lines and were wandering into the Muslim camp. The first assumption was that the men must be insane. On both encamping sides. The Christian soldiers might have added hatred of the mission to the thought. *There is nothing to discuss.* They were there for one purpose only. A crusade.

Perhaps Francis had a death wish. Many saints have spoken with zeal about the martyr's death. Teresa of Avila, for instance, talks in her autobiography of how she and her little brother used to play games in which they imagined themselves being gloriously martyred at the hands of infidels. She writes with the memory so fresh that it reads like it's a great pleasure to die.

Francis makes it clear that such a fate would have been fine with him too, but most of all, he was doing what he had first practiced with the leper who scared him at the beginning of his religious life. At first, revolted, he turned tail and left the begging leper behind him, disgusted by the sickness and filth, but then he spun around. He returned to the spot where the man stood, got off his horse, and embraced him. Earlier Francis had always fled people with this ailment—afraid of the alien, unexpected—but this time he walked up to the man, hugged and kissed him, and asked for forgiveness.

The time of the Crusades was full of stories told by Christians of the infidel, the Muslim leader with religious purpose prepared to destroy your Christian house and your Christian lands, raping and pillaging, and leading everyone you know away in chains. Then, as now, fear drove action, and anyone who wanted to "sell" you something (religion, patriotism, a crusade) knew to trigger you with fear as the prime motivator.

Francis was afraid too, but he knew that a God-lover was not supposed to allow fear to make decisions for him and that a Jesus-follower was to try to love everyone no matter what. It was not only the meeting that was scary. The travel to Damietta itself was scary. He'd tried to make the journey before; weather had forced him to turn back. The region wasn't unknown to Francis. Since the crusading era had been going on for a century already, the path had become somewhat well-worn, and he'd not only spoken to pilgrims who had been there before, but he had sent friars before to that ancient part of the world. Perhaps there was a sense of a different kind of adventure that turned the Crusades he'd entered earlier upside down. From war to peace as a purpose.

This is a point in Francis's life when the interpretation of what really happened in Egypt can turn on respect or disrespect for people of color. There is a long-standing explanation that turns on the notion that the darker-skinned people who met with the religious leader sent by God, who spoke of God, intended only to harm him. In visiting the sultan, was Francis there to perform miracles and triumph over the dark-skinned man, converting him and his nation of infidels to the true faith? Or was he there for the reason he gave, to meet in the only way that his own teacher, Jesus, had instructed a disciple to do: through love?

Releasing doves into the air is often made out to be the epigrammatic gesture of Francis of Assisi. But more than that are these moments when, fighting against his will, he refuses to be afraid. He refuses to remain in Assisi terrified of the faraway Arab Muslim and his different civilization. He refuses to give in to the ways that people in power want to frighten him and others.

Francis moved forward both vulnerable and wounded. There is no way he made it through that line of waiting crusading soldiers without receiving a kick or a strike or two. Remember, he was no saint then; he was only a beggar, a penitent and noncompliant fool, the sort of man whom fighting men hate. In fact, Francis strikes me as a man who throughout his adult life carried a wound. We will never know the scenes with his father that he never shared with anyone and that weren't carried out in public. Wounds were inflicted on him, and sometimes he inflicted them himself. I don't think he could have understood people without power as well as he seems to have otherwise. "A *Wounded* deer leaps highest," wrote Emily Dickinson.[1]

The Christian soldiers posed the greatest threat to his safety as he walked that line.

Ah look, a penitent in rags has come to save the world from evil!

He's a goddamn buffoon.

Strike his right cheek and see what he wants for the other one!

I may give him a penny for his cause in Rome,
but here I'll give him a kick in his bony ass!

The man that Sultan Malek al-Kamil saw approaching was a wounded man. This is why we hear that his first reaction was bemusement. *This is not going to be a negotiation. This is not a representative of Latin Christianity, unless it's a trick.* And it was no trick.

Al-Kamil was a peaceful man. He had already extended offers of negotiation, including the return of control of Jerusalem to the Christians, offers rebuffed by Cardinal Pelagius. He was also known to send food and water to Western soldiers after defeating them on the battlefield. He had been taught that these were among the humane ways of war.

Francis talked with al-Kamil (through interpreters, surely, though we don't have reliable written accounts), explaining why he was a follower of Jesus, and what Jesus taught his followers to do. I suspect that the sultan understood what Francis said very well. He was a scholar who appreciated Western culture, and he was a devout person too. That day, I suspect that they truly "met" one another.

Christians have long clung to a line from Saint Paul, "If you confess with your lips that Jesus is Lord and believe in your heart that God raised him from the dead, you will be saved" (Romans 10:9), with a missionary zeal that separates it from the rest of the teachings of Christian practice and witness. They want to say that it is belief and a certain kind of confession that matters, not anything else. But the "anything else," the *action* of a living faith, matters very much too.

Francis did both. He met words of faith with a life acting in faith. When he exchanged clothes with the beggar in Rome while he was on pilgrimage, he was putting himself in the thick of a problem. He'd just given money to support the church, which he knew helped take care of the poor, but that was not enough for him. He wanted to quite literally step into the other person's shoes.

You could imagine him today (and see yourself in solidarity with his mission), gathering with his group of followers in their scratchy, patched clothes standing as friends and allies to Black and brown and Indigenous communities in advocacy, peace, and protest, saying Black Lives Matter, Indigenous peoples and lands matter, our immigrant communities matter, and their lives matter and health care needs matter. You could translate his life path forward, imagining that he (and you, too) could confront religious leaders and leaders of nations who are caring for money and ideology before serving the people that they have been called to serve. You might see him—and you—living into the principles of faith and action you espouse, not only advocating for the needs of immigrants, but actually meeting with immigrants where you live and inviting them into your home. Breaking bread and offering solidarity.

It has become too easy to separate our living from our words, in ways that Francis could never have imagined. Both Francis and Clare of Assisi—the first woman who joined his way of life, and one of the most powerful ones ever to do so—had the words of Jesus, "Blessed are the humble," on their lips while facing their fears and when meeting those who frightened, threatened, or challenged them. We can take inspiration from the ways they physically and personally stepped into dangerous situations, not to be heroes, but to really understand what's going on and bring peace.

In the Hebrew Bible's book of Leviticus, the priest who makes a sacrifice in order to anoint and bless a person in need uses consecrated oil and places it on the earlobe, the thumb, and the big toe so that the anointed will viscerally remember to take care as to what they hear, what they carry, and where they go. Francis went about the world with that sense of anointing in his limbs and on his face. He also acted often as if the priest—or God—had pushed him from behind into the crowd of needs, saying, *Get out there.*

Chapter 6

WALK LIGHTLY ON THE GROUND

No one ever talks about a vow of poverty as an expression of love for others, but for Francis it was, and for us it can be. Willingly choosing to consume, hold, and use less of the resources available to all of us—as expressed when someone vows to live poorly—is a way of affirming the value of others. And by living poorly I mean being willing to live with less or being conscious of living with only what you need. The pope who first took the name Francis was also the one to write an encyclical subtitled "On care for our common home." He said, "The natural environment is a collective good, the patrimony of all humanity and the responsibility of everyone. If we make something our own, it is only to administer it for the good of all. If we do not, we burden our consciences with the weight of having denied the existence of others. That is why the New Zealand bishops asked what the commandment 'Thou shalt not kill' means when 'twenty percent of the world's population consumes resources at a rate that robs the poor nations and future generations of what they need to survive.'"[1]

It may seem strange to us today, but imagine how much stranger it must have appeared to people eight hundred years ago when Francis practiced gentleness, growing flowers in the garden that he never picked, walking carefully over rocks, returning captured animals to the wild, and reverently touching ordinary things. To him, nothing was truly inanimate; nothing one encountered was uncreated, and so nothing was to be handled roughly.

Francis saw a direct correlation between an unconverted life and rough, inconsiderate living.

What he practiced wasn't what we often call mindfulness today, what Hugh Prather, a bestselling self-help writer of the 1970s, beautifully described: "Those who walk in gentleness walk upon holy ground," meaning that we make our places holy by how we treat them. Likewise, the practice of mindfulness, native most of all to Zen, teaches this. While good, this differs from Francis's way. Francis wasn't gentle in order to make the path holy. He was more like an Indigenous person who understands the created world—the world under our feet—as inherently holy. He didn't have to make it so. It was holy. It is already holy.

Francis would have stood in agreement with the concerns of Luther Standing Bear, a Lakota leader from a century ago who explained why the white person's approach of dominating creation was foreign to him: "We did not think of the great open plains, the beautiful rolling hills, the winding streams with tangled growth, as *wild*. Only to the white man was nature a *wilderness* and only to him was it *infested* with *wild* animals and *savage* people. To us it was tame. Earth was bountiful and we were surrounded with the blessings of the Great Mystery."[2]

Understood by many Indigenous traditions over time, the connection Francis felt with nonhuman creatures and the earth itself was considered strange in his time and remains uncanny even in ours. How often do we hear of a Christian exemplar who cares to aid the worms who wash up on the road after a storm, relocating them? We have accounts of Francis doing even this. In these ways, again, his care and approach come close in comparison to First Nation and Indigenous people who have long understood the gifts of, and felt kinship with, animals, insects, seasons, and birds, and perhaps even nonarthropod invertebrates and the rest of the created world.

His gentleness also was not romantic. He was not like William Blake, the Romantic poet, suggesting that virtue is rooted in innocence only to be later destroyed by experience. Gentleness was Francis's moral code, and his ethics were intentional. Look again at the most pious original accounts of the encounters marking his path of conversion and you see him struggling to do what is right. You see a conflicted will at work— like when he passes that leper on the street, unfeeling and uncaring, but then turns back, with feeling and care and embrace, to find him. He was always turning around, which is what "conversion" speaks to.

Gentleness was rooted in his powerlessness, which Francis took also to mean literal smallness. To be diminutive was to rebuke what we usually try to make of ourselves: we who always strive to be stronger, more influential, and more important, or at least pretend to be. Humans are the only species that writes history. We are also the only species that puts ourselves at the center of everything. As if the entire universe exists so that we may each spend about eighty years on this single planet.

He is the bird bath saint, but forget that image. Instead, consider Francis as someone who understood that animals, birds, and insects can find their way home in situations when humans never possibly could. He knew that such creatures recognize faces, know one another by smell and instinct, and he felt kinship with them at this level. He wasn't sitting with birds perched on his fingers as an end-all; he was watching them, wondering at their qualities, and learning from them.

His responses to animals, birds, and bugs are not what we've come to expect from human relationships with other creatures in our own day. He didn't seek to domesticate creatures, for instance, and he didn't use them for his own purposes. His connections to creatures were of the native sort. In fact, he wrote this in his *Rule*, which was written for all the men who had joined him as friars: "I command all the brothers, both clergy and laity, when they travel about the world, or reside in various places, that they never have animals with them, or entrust an animal to the care of others, or in any other way keep one."[3] There were no pets in the early friaries. No cats on the lap or dogs on the hearth. None "used" for transportation, except for those who were infirm.

Most striking was his relationship with birds, when he "preached" to them on the road. Most humans have so little relationship to bird life. We may know them by sight. We put up bird houses and feeders and identify their species with the help of guidebooks. But it isn't as if birds lie homeless or die hungry without our help. Our gestures are mostly for the purpose of drawing them nearer so that we may see them and feel that we are participating in their lives, which are so different from our own.

When Francis first preached to birds—which is often the first thing that most people learn about him—it was during a time of personal uncertainty. He was wandering outside the city into the fields, and he stopped, seeing an avian congregation. He stopped and inexplicably began to preach. Really? "Preach"? It seems so. Thomas of Celano reports, "From that day on, he carefully exhorted all birds, all animals, all reptiles, and also insensible creatures, to praise and love the creator."[4] How strange this must have seemed to those around him.

There's the son of Bernardone coming back again from the hills. Did you hear that he now preaches to the birds?

Well, of course. No one in Assisi wants to listen to him.

But to birds? Surely he can find an audience with the lepers in the valley.

They'll listen as long as he brings them food and water.

The birds can have him!

He seems to have known animals, birds, and bugs for what and who they were. For example, the otherwise inconspicuous wren—which appears in the famous Giotto painting that hangs in the basilica in Assisi of that first preaching event—when beginning its spring calling is so boisterous that it nearly shatters an otherwise contemplative moment. But what do we know about wren music or bird conversation—perhaps it is another contemplative voice? Likewise, the swallows that glide just above the surface of the lake, dipping and diving, are amazing to watch. They are also feeding. Their acrobatics are not for our benefit. For all we know, a swoop of swallows is known to the avian world more like a dread squadron than a troupe of elegant dancers. Maybe Francis recognized what he could not possibly "know" about them.

Most startling is this passage from his first biographer, Brother Thomas of Celano:

Even for worms he had a warm love, since he had read this text about the Savior: *I am a worm and not a man.* That is why he used to pick them up from the road and put them in a safe place so that they would not be crushed by the footsteps of passersby.

What shall I say about the other lesser creatures? In the winter he had honey or the best wine put out for the bees so that they would not perish from the cold. He used to extol the artistry of their work and their remarkable ingenuity, giving glory to the Lord. With such an outpouring, he often used up an entire day or more in praise of them and other creatures. Once the three young men *in the furnace of burning fire* invited all the elements *to praise and glorify* the Creator of all things, so this *man, full of the spirit of God* never stopped *glorifying, praising, and blessing* the Creator and Ruler of all things in all the elements and creatures.

How great do you think was the delight the beauty of flowers brought to his soul whenever he glimpsed their forms and took in their fragrances? He would immediately turn his gaze to the beauty of that flower, brilliant in springtime, sprouting *from the root of Jesse.* By its *fragrance* it raised up countless thousands of the dead. Whenever he found an abundance of flowers, he used to preach to them and invite them to praise the Lord, just as if they were endowed with reason.[5]

Brother Thomas may have been overeager to give these odd behaviors a basis in Holy Scripture, but still, how beautiful this is!

Just a few lines down from those, the poet Thomas styles this conclusion to the scene in verse:

Finally, he used to call all creatures
by the name of "brother" and "sister"
and in a wonderful way, unknown to others,
he could discern the *secrets of the heart* of
    creatures
like someone who has already passed
*into the freedom of the glory of the children
    of God.*[6]

Maybe natural reasons explain the skill of Francis to know the hearts of nonhuman creatures better than spiritual ones do, but I won't douse this biographer's enthusiasm for what he witnessed.

Some might ask if walking gently on the earth included plants. Francis experts rarely pause to consider them, because Francis only spoke of flowers, and we also haven't understood plants in that realm of communication very well until quite recently. Not long ago, a French philosopher offered this reflection, elliptically describing what plants do that is particularly extraordinary: "To cling to the surface of the Earth to better penetrate the air and the ground. To moor at random and then to expose and open oneself to anything in the surrounding world, regardless of its form or nature. Never to move, in order to allow for the world to be swallowed up in one's breast all the more."[7] What the philosopher noted might have been echoed by Francis: they use the sun and air to create nourishment for themselves and others, taking or asking nothing in return. Flowers may be the only plants that Francis took note of, according to the records we have of him, but he likely grasped that they possess a natural humility that surpasses human attempts at the same.

Given what we know about the attitudes of medieval people toward nonhuman species, combined with saints' legacies as crafted by the hagiographers, it's safe to assume that for every anecdote of this strange sort—Francis walking gently over stones or exhorting flowers—preserved in the earliest biographies, there must be many others excised by his contemporaries or successors seeking to avoid scandal. Francis's reverence for plants and animals was absolutely shocking.

The poet Rainer Maria Rilke once wrote in a letter, talking about great sculpture, "the stones of ancient cultures were not calm,"[8] suggesting that a sculpted work is ready to become art before a chisel ever touches it. The stone itself is already full of life. The sculptor's skill brings out of a living stone what was there all along. I don't know if Francis ever saw great sculpture, but he had this artist's view of the living quality of the medium.

Another early twentieth-century artist, Wassily Kandinsky, in *Concerning the Spiritual in Art*, wrote of the artist Paul Cezanne that he "was endowed with the gift of divining the inner life in everything."[9] This manifested itself in the still-life paintings Cezanne was creating, giving life to things like a sugar bowl, a tree, and pieces of fruit. With his brush he tried to show that each thing, inanimate or not, *breathed*. Francis looked at the world in this mystical way too.

Perhaps he knew the stories of stones from holy scripture: how it was a stone upon which Jacob rested his head all night while he dreamed of angels descending and ascending on a stairway. There was the stone that Goliath used to slay the giant. A stone featured prominently when Daniel interpreted King Nebuchadnezzar's dream by smashing into a statue. Then there were the stones the crowd used to murder Saint Stephen, the first Christian martyr and probably the first catechist of the faith. And the animating life that Jesus spoke of when he said that even the stones cry out.

In his feet gently moving over the created earth, in his consideration of the birds, the flowers, the sun, the moon, and the stones of the earth, Francis still teaches us. Most of all, I see Francis's habits and attitude as part of his humility—something we need to recover. The earth's resources are to be shared among its inhabitants and sustained by careful attention. Whether it is vertebrates, invertebrates, fish, plants, or stones, when we reorient ourselves and look truthfully at things as they are, we realize how tangential we become to the enterprise of all that is—certainly of all that we can know and experience—because "the world is the breath of the living" and is not defined by our presence and experience.[10]

Chapter 7

REFUSE POWER

Francis lived in a time and place when a person could easily come to know intimate details about everyone in their town or village. Those of us for whom years may go by without knowing the names of our next-door neighbors will have trouble imagining this. But in the early thirteenth century, there really was no *speed*: nothing faster than a horse, usually at a clip-clop, and almost no one owned a horse. If you heard horses' hooves, chances were good that a wealthy landowner was paying a visit, or a bishop was passing through.

At the other end of the spectrum from speed, when you move slowly—at a walking pace—everywhere you go, you have the opportunity to see much more. You come to know each house, each field, and every stream and its banks as you prepare to cross it, again and again. You also end up meeting people and knowing them in ways that seem odd or quaint to us now.

Within ten years of Francis's first public gestures of converted life, the number of friars who joined his band increased to five or six thousand souls, and they were located in several countries. This was growth beyond all imagining. Pope Innocent III, from Rome, had granted simple permission to Francis to live a life of repentance and to preach the same to others. What harm could it do? But then, *five thousand* friars? That could be trouble.

He's a man in rags, Holy Father. What harm can come of it?

Men in rags with holy intentions often become men of influence.

But Your Holiness, influential among whom? Others who want to live a life of penitence and submission to the will of God? This can only be good for the Holy See.

We shall see.

Many of these followers of Francis were young, and many of them hadn't walked beside Francis in the early days, learning personally from him. They soon wanted to make changes.

They wanted to be called upon to do good work, inviting connections with other religious orders and with the curia in Rome. And they wanted a sense of place. They would have no power in the world as long as they had no permanent places or houses of their own. The little chapels they'd restored were for other priests and religious orders. They needed real churches of their own, with convents with their names on them, and schools where young recruits could be sent for education toward ordination in the Franciscan way.

They wanted education. Francis warned against book learning. It would create pride, he said, and possibly get in the way of spiritual practice. For developing a heart for God, books are at best a second-best way, but they're good because we know how to use them. This is why Francis asked every friar to do some work with his hands, not for money, but for the sake of his soul. Each friar should get out of their head each day for a period of time. But for many, to become professors at the great universities popping up in western Europe at that time became a goal. A professor was a "master" with students. Then they could show the other religious orders that Franciscans had brains too, not just deeds.

Many also wanted priestly ordination, something that Francis had been ambivalent about. He desperately wanted his brothers to avoid elevated status of any kind, including to the priesthood when possible, because he said that they were most of all called to humility. His name for their religious brotherhood, after all, was *Friars Minor*, which means, little (or "lesser" or "junior") brothers, and he took the *minor* seriously.

Even the itinerancy of the early preaching of Francis was risky to the status quo. Licensed preachers outside the normal clergy and churches might say something that challenges or contradicts a local priest or bishop. There were those who were keeping a close eye and ear on what Francis was saying. And because Francis's influence on people was profound and unique in that first decade, soon a bishop, then a cardinal, was appointed to "protect" the young religious order, as a kind of "hall monitor" for the church.

Francis·was about the Umbrian and Tuscan countryside in his century like the Baul poets and singers once were a century ago in Bengal. *Baul* means "possessed of wind," where this use of "wind" related to an intentional blend of breath, air, and spirit—like *pneuma* in ancient Greek and *ruach* in Hebrew. Baul songs were a kind of preaching, as early Franciscan preaching was really a kind of singing for God.

The early preaching of Francis and his friends was meant to be dangerous: to easy assumptions, to the status quo, and to a life without spirit. The following words from a Baul song of fifty years ago could easily translate into Francis's language from eight hundred years ago: "If you want to conquer your spirit, form a gang of bandits; use devotion as your pivot, and break into the house of dharma."[1] *Dharma* means religious teaching or the house of established faith. In those earliest days, Francis was quietly, with his gang of bandits, showing people how to find their spirit-wind by quiet insurrection.

To refuse power takes many forms, and they are nearly always quiet. The one who boldly refuses power does not refuse it at all. For this reason, it's important, in Francis's case, to take note of what we *don't* hear of him doing. He did not, for instance, record his dreams. He did not speak to anyone of private revelations from God, beyond the most basic beginning in his religious life—that moment in crumbling old San Damiano when he heard, "Go, rebuild my church." And he didn't even tell his closest friends about the revelation of a seraph-shaped Christ in the sky that came to him and imprinted him with stigmata wounds. Which is why we'll leave that scene alone, because that's precisely where he left it.

Francis refused to be powerful in ways that most people seeking power go after it. Instead, people were drawn to him for what was an authentic charisma and spirit, no doubt from God.

He remained an obedient son of the Catholic Church and always honored those who were ordained. But he also understood their weaknesses and believed that he and others were in the church for a reason: "We have been sent to help clerics for the salvation of souls, that we may supply whatever may be found wanting in them," he said.[2] Then he adds, "Everyone will receive his reward [in the afterlife], but not according to his authority, rather according to the work he performs." This didn't make bishops and popes happy, and the frequent-seeming ease with which the church has made popes into saints argues that Francis's teaching on this matter has not been widely accepted or followed. He even speaks of some clergy "hinder[ing] the salvation of people," promising that when this happens, God will punish them for the harm that they do.[3]

These differences all came to a bursting point by the time Francis returned from his famous meeting with the sultan in Egypt. Arriving back in Assisi, Francis realized how far away he had been from the daily work of the order. The long travels to Egypt had brought schism to the Friars Minor. Seeing all that had changed and erupted, he stepped down from leadership. The movement he had unintentionally founded had become too large, unmanageable by the original ideals and through the intimate ways in which it had grown. So Francis decided to let someone else lead. He remained involved, preaching and teaching, attending meetings, even asking permission of the new leaders to speak, but he was glad to let go of leadership, knowing that power often changes us in negative ways, harming us and harming others.

He was like the monk who briefly ruled the church at the other end of the thirteenth century, Pope Celestine V, who willingly resigned as pontiff because he wanted nothing to do with the reins of power. He found himself the head of something of which he did not approve. For Francis, the difference between living a distinctive way of following

Christ and inspiring others who want to do that, too, was hugely different from being the minister-general of a large international enterprise.

For him, the rabbi-savior Jesus's words remained the only important words of his spiritual direction. These included "Truly I tell you, unless you change and become like children, you will never enter the kingdom of heaven" (Matthew 18:3). Five thousand friars or not, there was no sophistication that he found necessary and no religious appointment that could accomplish what he felt called by God to do.

Chapter 8

LISTEN TO YOUR INNER ANIMAL

The records of those pious lives of saints often praise the way in which those saints were "dead" to the world as their lives went on, as if they were leaving the material world behind and only inhabiting a kind of spiritual realm. In Francis, though, matter and spirit closely and meaningfully mingled from beginning to end. I have no doubt that in his conversion he curbed those "worldly" things like lust, greed, and laziness, because each was in his early life but faded as he himself changed. But he did not "put a curb upon his senses," as one early account puts it.[1] He would never disdain the created world.

Instead, as his life went on, his senses took in more and more. He saw and heard and touched the world in ways he couldn't imagine having done earlier. And it wasn't that he saw angels in the trees, or the prophet Elijah charioting across the sky; he now saw birds in the trees that before he would have missed, and he observed the wind's movement and felt kinship with the sun in ways that left him at times breathless with wonder while observing the sky.

We know these things about him because we have his own writings, in which the wild world is praised and compared to the ways of God. Creatures are called his "sisters" and "brothers." We also have multiple accounts of long retreats that Francis went on alone in the mountains.

These accounts often indicate that his friends were nearby—but not too close to Francis—since he asked them to leave him alone at various times.

Have you seen him today? I haven't.

Yes. What do you think he is doing?

He's up there all alone, without even books or food.

Could it be that he isn't hungry or thirsty?

For a week at a time?

Perhaps.

I don't know.

I guess he'll return when he's ready.

Maybe I will keep an eye on him from a distance, anyway.

Francis seemed to grasp the essential solitude of a life well lived. He knew that each of us on our deathbed, even if friends are all around, is dying alone. He also grasped that we also ultimately live alone, and we must become comfortable in our aloneness and being alone with the Alone.

Most of Francis's miracles were ordinary and not the usual pious, saint-chronicled sort. Unlike Saint Paul, Francis didn't have visions of Christ on the road. But what he met on the road he welcomed, like the robbers whose threats couldn't really faze him. On that day, Francis was singing French songs while walking by himself when a group of lawless bandits approached and threatened him. *You fool. Give us everything you have.* Bandits were a common occurrence on the unprotected roads of Italy in the Middle Ages. When he was stopped, Francis of course had nothing on him, which made the men angry. They began to rough him up and rip his already patched clothing. *There's nothing you can really take from me*, Francis essentially told them. He was a fool, but one who saw more than anyone imagined.

Francis met the wolf, met the bandits, and met the leper on their own terms. He met each one and spoke to the moment: To the wolf, he heard the hunger. To the bandits, he spoke to what they wanted to steal and pointed to something inside himself that could not be stolen. Meeting the leper, he met his own fear, his own inner animal, and turned it back, turning again to the leper, embracing him.

The lesson of meeting who we are, and who other creatures are, on common ground is something I've considered often in my life. About twenty years ago, I lived with my family in a log cabin in the woods of Vermont. There were rumors of a black bear from a generation earlier, neighbors informed us. But all we saw were deer, an occasional moose, bats at dusk, owls at night, and wild turkeys all year round. But we didn't see a bear on our hill.

Once, when I bought rabbits for each of my children, housing them in a five-foot hutch at the edge of the yard, the bunnies seemed happy and fine the first day and night. On morning number two, thankfully unseen by the kids, alone out there in the dark, some creature had pulled apart the meshing of the hutch and snatched the rabbits away. I found blood and no bunnies, and I lied to my kids. "I think they've escaped into the woods," I cheerily told them. But I don't think that was a bear.

Soon after the rabbits, we adopted two domesticated cats. One of which was unforgettable in her refusal to remain domesticated.

This cat came to us with the name Bowie-hena, from the Hebrew (my coworker was Jewish) בוא הנה, meaning "Come here." She was declawed, a so-called house cat, but the moment we brought her to our log cabin it was clear that she had other ideas in mind. When one of us would open the door, even a crack, Bowie was there trying—successfully—to bolt into the sunlight.

Every day, for the first two weeks, we ran after her into the woods to catch and carry her back inside. We were anxious to care for our new animals and lived with the fear of the harm of bears and other creatures in the night. Daily we would follow her through the woods and undergrowth, swiping away branches, frantically calling her name.

On about the fifteenth day of doing this, I was exhausted. Also, it was ridiculous. "If she's going to be eaten by wolves or a bear, so be it. This cat refuses to live indoors!" From that moment, we reluctantly allowed Bowie to freely go in and out.

I expected she'd probably be dead within a week. The cat had been an indoor cat in a condo, not in the woods. I assumed Bowie must have no idea what she was getting herself into. I was wrong. This is what she was designed to do. Declawed and all, in the middle of the woods of Vermont, with those creatures and every bump in the night, it turned out that Bowie-hena came and went at her leisure and lived another twelve years.

I thought of Saint Francis when Bowie came to live with us because I remembered how Francis did not approve of having pets. He didn't want to see animals domesticated. He loved the wildness of creatures— what he saw as their natural ways—and asked his fellow friars to leave animals where they were.

He always honored that which was wild in the Alone within creation. Once, when a fisherman had Francis out in his boat and he caught a particularly big fish, he handed it as a gift to the saint. Francis kissed it and sent it back into the water. More famous is the story of Francis's first gestures as a convert to religious life. He purchased caged birds at the market and then released them into the air. He always felt that the freedom of birds to fly and to sing was what God intended.

He also found that God-intended wildness in himself. He spent long periods of time in the wilderness. The scenes of his life are not scenes of Francis in a monastery or sitting for very long in a church. But of outdoor spaces, lonely caves, near trees. After he left his father and the townspeople, he began sleeping in abandoned churches, but that period of his life did not last long. The next scenes of his life are transitioning to the mountains, or caves, or the woods. He exchanged the cultivated, civilized ways of his childhood with more native ways and places to find and communicate with God.

Fast forward many years now. Bowie is gone but has left me with valuable lessons from her and from Francis. I live in Wisconsin, where I still spend a good deal of time in the woods, near a lake. Last winter, in the weeks before spring when the lake was still half-covered with ice, we saw the Sandhill Cranes beginning to arrive. On the first day, my daughter and I walked onto the mostly still-frozen surface and as two of the cranes barked at us, we pulled out our kayaks, approaching them slowly for a closer look, their long legs moving deliberately on the near-frozen mud of the shore.

They were not pleased with this. They then flapped those very long wings into action, flying away.

The next day, we repeated the process, hoping to watch the cranes again, so beautiful and rare. They summer in these parts, where large tracts of quiet farmland are found beside small lakes and rivers. In slightly secluded spots around the lake we somewhat stealthily followed them.

On the third day, the Sandhill Cranes were gone, apparently for good. I have no doubt we in fact scared them away. In our curiosity to see and know and appreciate their wild ways, we sent them away to someplace quieter and wilder.

Again I thought of Francis. I'd forgotten his teachings on wildness, and my forgetfulness had hurt me and others. So now I will try to do better.

Francis, meeting the Alone and his own aloneness in that cave, learned his own lessons about what was wild within him. And for the rest of his life, he refused to tame what was wild, refused to dissect the wildness of his experience of God. As I reflect on the wild way of Francis, there are moments when I'm present, trying to nest, and my soul needs to be able to settle in without feeling the need to show and record and explain itself to anyone else paddling nearby to look, without explaining itself even to me.

Chapter 9

HAVE NOTHING
TO LOSE

We want to be with you and do what you're doing. Tell us what we should do with our possessions. That's what two men said to Francis after watching his public confessions and demonstrations of penance. Similar words would be echoed by many others from that day forward.

Even the question is astounding. For those who not only observed the moment in the town square but paid attention to Francis, it was clear that to follow in his footsteps, you couldn't do what he was doing while holding on to stuff.

No statement of belief was required. The first and only thing a person had to do was agree to go home and give away all their possessions. It was a statement of obedience that Francis declared. And it echoed the words of Jesus to the young rich man in the Gospel of Mark (10:20–22), words that offered a kind of freedom.

The simplicity of Francis's response to the first two men who asked the question—Bernard of Quinta-valle and Peter Catanii—is wonderful. When they ask how they can join him in this work, Francis responds, "Let us go and seek counsel from the Lord."[1] This is not your parents' religious leader. These are words that do not come from a sense of law, protocol, or tradition. Francis assumes no authority at all in his response. The three men then walk together to a nearby church and kneel and pray.

In the church, a priest who is formally educated and able to read reads a Gospel text in Latin (the exclusive language of church readings of scripture at that time). He helps them find various gospel texts: Mark 10:21, Matthew 16:24, and Luke 9:3 in the missal, each a passage that reveals Jesus's instructions to his own disciples. These become the foundation for all that follows:

> "Go, sell what you own, and give the money to the poor."

"If any want to become my followers, let them deny themselves and take up their cross and follow me."

"Take nothing for your journey, no staff, nor bag, nor bread, nor money—not even an extra tunic."

It would be much easier to become a Benedictine, I imagine Bernard and Peter saying to each other.

I'd gladly vow to avoid women for the rest of my life. It is easier to say yes to chastity.

And yes to poverty too.

And yes to obedience. It is God's will.

But this . . . this seems rather . . . unclear?

What will we do next?

We don't know.

Bernard has a lot to give up; we're told that he was one of the wealthiest people in town. Peter has comparatively little to lose; at least, this is the usual way of interpreting the scene. But we might consider it differently: that as a wealthy man who lived alone Bernard was perhaps the neediest of people. And Peter, who was without worries but had many friends, younger with fewer commitments, found it easier than the rich man to follow in the steps of their friend who wanted to go through the world without material possessions.

This new way of being in the world wasn't only about not owning things. It was also about moving around in the world as if you don't own things. As if you had no interest in protecting your things.

Despite such teachings about material possessions, Francis always also insisted that each friar work hard each day, in support of their community and because work was considered good in itself, and its own spiritual discipline. Perhaps you've heard the Sicilian folktale of Jesus and Saint Peter and the stones that turn to bread. It's a story that easily could have been written by an experienced Franciscan.

The story goes that Jesus and the disciples are walking in a place where there's no food and they're all gradually feeling ravenous. Jesus says to everyone, pick up a stone and carry it with you. A strange instruction, but who is going to question their master? Each disciple picks up a stone, Peter choosing the smallest one he can find. It was hot, after all, that day, and stones are heavy. Sometime later, they arrive at a place where it is good to rest and Jesus says to everyone again, now hold out your stones and I will bless them, and you'll each have bread to eat. So Christ blesses them, and each man sees that he is no longer holding a stone but has a loaf the size of his stone. Peter was furious.[2] The tale deems his laziness and irresponsibility incongruous with living lightly.

In most of the early accounts, Francis seemed joyful in direct proportion to how separated he was from what other people valued: money. For example, when Giles, the third person to join the small band of those without possessions, imitates Francis by giving everything he possessed away, he then joins Francis's company as the two walk the road toward the Marches of Ancona, a beautiful and somewhat remote part of the Italian peninsula. Francis, we're told, began to sing French songs along the way. The men, it says, "were filled with great joy." Why, exactly? "They regarded as bitter what people of the world consider desirable."

Money, to Francis, was like treasure in a pirate ship; it was nearly always ill-gotten, wrong to hold onto, and an encumbrance to quick sailing. At that time, a person could rarely have riches without trampling on those who have little. Masters had serfs. Knights had servants. Ownership of property was reserved only for the privileged.

Also, property had to be fiercely defended. There really wasn't a middle class, not yet, although Francis's father's business was on the cusp of this. But Francis could only see money as one of the "things that bring about much misery and grief" (that's how the sentence quoted two paragraphs above finishes). We are closer to this situation now than we may think.

I realize that what I like most about "my things"— even and especially the mundane and inexpensive things, like old books, special photographs, my bicycle and kayak—is the way they make me feel in control of my surroundings. Like a character's experience of being comfortable in a familiar cave in Percival Everett's novel *Telephone*, with these things I've been in a "place that I knew more about than anyone else." They comfort me in that way. To Francis, that would be all the more reason to let them go: where comfort and control have as real a hold as the possessions themselves.

In 1208, Francis traveled to a tiny town in the Valley of Rieti, north of Assisi, and for the first time began greeting strangers by saying, *"Buon giorno, buona gente*" (Good morning, good people). He was a young penitent in rags with a smile on his face. The people there would always remember his salutation as a gesture of uncommon generosity and openness. Soon this greeting became a hallmark of walking the Way of Francis. His friars thereafter would often say upon arriving or passing through somewhere, "*Buon giorno, buona gente!*" And the people knew that these people entering their town were gentle people in a crass and violent time.

A couple years earlier, there was that incident when he had been walking alone through a wood, surely with that same innocent joyfulness on his face, only this time he was singing, in French. It was common for thieves and outlaws to hide or live in the woods, away from the roads, far from towns where they might be found. (Think: Robin Hood.) These thieves saw the silly man singing his lungs out and they came upon him, menacingly, demanding all that he had.

He of course had nothing on him. No one can steal from you what you do not possess, and from the look of him, there was no ransom to be had either.

Another account of that incident adds more details. "Who are you?" they demanded.

Caught up in the moment as he was, Francis looked at the thieves and said, "I'm a herald of the

Great King. And what is it to you?" For the insolence, they gave him a knock on the head and threw him down a hill into a giant bank of snow. No one has time for fools, but as Regan says in *King Lear*, "Jesters do oft prove prophets."

Over the course of Francis's life, more than five thousand people came to follow the Franciscan way; a movement grew from one to five thousand in less than twenty years. With so many people, it became impractical for all of them to live so simply. Francis decided to take those portions of the teachings of Jesus at face value and truly not worry about tomorrow. He did no planning. There was no thought about tomorrow. There was a freedom to this that appealed to those thousands of people, but the decision also undid him, and the movement itself.

Even during Francis's lifetime, practices of having nothing, or planning nothing, became controversial. They were impractical to a fault. For example, how would it be possible to train young men to be knowledgeable Franciscans without providing them with books or places of study, let alone reliable roofs over their heads?

At the time Francis was away in the Nile Delta, a split originated in the religious order over the commitment to poverty. Some friars openly questioned the notion that Jesus lived in poverty. Were they as friars imitating Jesus in something that wasn't true? Others made a more practical assertion: that they couldn't continue this way, as their numbers grew—that they had to become like other religious orders with houses, schools, security, money in the bank, and resources upon which they might build the future. Less than a century after Francis's death, when this conflict reached its absolute peak, Pope John XXII took sides, declaring that anyone who taught that Jesus lived in the kind of poverty that Francis of Assisi taught and lived in was a heretic. Some friars were then murdered by their religious brothers for holding fast to Francis's teaching.

"Walking by faith rather than by human prudence" is the simple and accurate way one Franciscan author has explained what Francis so controversially did.[3] It's probably safe to assume that really no one, and no religious community, fully does this in the same way today. Francis was simple and naive on purpose. Mortgages, rent, and bank loans are evidence against this approach. Even soaking beans as preparation for tomorrow's supper—a habit that Francis once rebuked one cooking friar for doing—argues against it. Not that God would soften the beans miraculously, but perhaps the beans were fine without softening, and the soaking of beans would only lead to more planning and more elaborate "requirements" for meal preparations tomorrow.

We are not satisfied with little, or with less than what we feel we deserve. Sometimes our spiritual teachers even encourage these feelings of entitlement, as if they come from holy places. They don't. Francis knew better. Those of us who want to follow his wisdom might refocus our lives to avoid the issues and heartbreak that arise when we stray far from the simplicity for which we were made. Desires that lead to excess, misplaced concern, and ownership too often harm our faith and harm others. A Franciscan in the twenty-first century holds possessions lightly and shares them easily.

Chapter 10

SPEND TIME
IN THE WOODS

It is such a small thing, and perhaps I shouldn't make so much of it, but in the early chapters of one of the first biographies of Francis, he is described as delivering a little homily. A few months into the whole Franciscan way of life movement, when their company numbered only seven, this is what we see: "Calling together his six brothers in the woods next to the church of Saint Mary of the Portiuncula where they often went to pray, he told them: 'My dear brothers, let us consider our calling because God has mercifully called us not only for our own good but also for the salvation of many.'"[1] It's that first half of the first sentence I'm pointing toward. Look at where he pulled them before he began to speak: into the woods next to the church, not in the church itself.

This is a small thing, I suppose, but it indicates something that the usual commentators don't ever point to: How can we imagine how Francis came to appreciate the birds to which, they like to remind us, he preached to? I don't think Francis was preaching simply to be heard, or that it was his purpose to scold the creatures of the air (as if they ought to be praising their Creator, and shouldn't they already know it), as is often described in the accounts. The evidence points instead to a man who came to understand indigenous, natural things, and this would include trees, bird habits and bird calls, and the land itself.

If early paintings of the scene are accurate, then there were a lot of wrens in the trees when Francis was preaching to the birds. One popular early guide to identification, *A Field Guide to Western Birds*, poetically described the call of the wren as "a gushing cadence of clear curved notes tripping down the scale."[2] In fact, many bird-watchers have noted, and perhaps you have noticed yourself, how the wren's voice out-scales its tiny size. I'll bet that Francis understood these subtleties because he listened carefully and watched what birds do and even how they speak, call, and sing. He didn't simply intrude on their singing one day and preach at them.

Birds are to Francis's Umbria as rivers were to William Wordsworth's Lake District—the essential natural backdrop of a poet's life. The Romantic Wordsworth began his autobiographical poem, *The Prelude*, with opening lines of how the Derwent River's "murmurs" and "rocky falls" and "shallows, sent a voice / That flow'd along my dreams" with "ceaseless music." I think the birds of Umbria were the equivalent formation for Francis and that the joy and music of Umbrian birds burst from him in his maturity.

We have many stories of Francis being close to birds, wolves, bugs, fish, and rabbits. Beyond the sweet gentleness of these anecdotes, there is something more. He was paying attention to the rhythms and ways of the natural world—ways of life that are both more elementary and more essential than our twenty-first-century ones.

In gospel texts, Jesus, of course, praised nature, spent time alone in the hills, in the desert, by the water, on the water. He took particular praise of the lilies of the field for not toiling or spinning, as the Authorized Version once put it, or without overwork or worry. Ever since Sunday school I've understood this passage in the gospels as about beautiful flowers not worrying. It was as if a smile on one's face, like a flower in bloom, could erase the pain of a difficult life. What a contrivance that was, gleaned from whoever taught it to me.

Reading the gospels, can you imagine Jesus teaching such a thing? Now, I can't either.

You can't grasp the lilies of the field without more fundamentally recognizing them as plants. Genus before species. Could the patient quality that Jesus was praising have been behind his holding up those simple, silent plants as exemplary, long before a thirteenth-century Francis offered a similar attention? And long before a twenty-first-century French philosopher put it this way? "[Plants] have no selective relation to what surrounds them: they are, and cannot be other than, constantly exposed to the world around them. Plant life is life as complete exposure, in absolute continuity and total communion with the environment. . . . Their absence of movement is nothing but the reverse of their complete adhesion to what happens to them and their environment. One cannot separate the plant . . . from the world that accommodates it. It is the most intense, radical, and paradigmatic form of being in the world."[3] All plants exhibit these qualities. Oak trees, daylilies, and switchgrass all communicate lessons of humility and communion more than any other created thing can do.

Near our house in rural Wisconsin is an ancient oak tree that I find myself talking with from time to time. I think it is Saint Francis who first gave me permission to do something as odd as talk with a wise tree, but it isn't a stray impulse of mine to do so. It is a desire to learn a different language that has me talking to trees, and most of all, listening to them.

Botanist and member of the Citizen Potawatomi Nation Robin Wall Kimmerer says in *Braiding Sweetgrass*, "I come here to listen, to nestle in the curve of the roots in a soft hollow of pine needles, to lean my bones against the column of white pine, to turn off the voice in my head until I can hear the voices outside it: the *shhh* of wind in needles, water trickling over rock, nuthatch tapping, chipmunks digging, beechnut falling, mosquito in my ear, and something more—something that is not me, for which we have no language, the wordless being of others in which we are never alone."[4]

Francis didn't exactly speak to trees, according to the early accounts. He didn't even mention them by their species names, but we see him often walking in the woods, choosing sylvan canopies under which to pray or under which to instruct his brothers, where we meet him. "Calling together his six brothers in the woods next to the church of Saint Mary of the Portiuncula where they often went to pray, he told them . . ."

Why are we gathering here, outside the church?

Isn't the chapel the place we ought to be praying?

Yes. It is in there where God has spoken to Brother Francis, telling him what to do.

Isn't it also there where we find God's presence in the holy sacrament?

I think so.

Francis wasn't sentimental when it came to the woods or when it came to relating to other creatures of the earth, generally. Despite a popular trope that originated in the 1970s, Francis was no hippie. What he discovered in the woods proved to be literal and true, not metaphoric.

Fully present in the present, Francis seems to have paid little attention to the past. He wasn't remembering what might have happened in the shade of those trees centuries earlier. Sentimentality cannot exist without yearning for something "lost." All that Francis had lost, he had thrown aside. He had a gift for seeing only today, of living in the present moment. So why do we sentimentalize him so much when we talk of him talking with birds and creatures?

Animal tales did not originate with Francis, nor did they even begin in Italy. We find Saint Cuthbert and his eider ducks in Northumberland and Saint Modomnoc and his bees in Ireland, both relatively well known. There was also a lay saint in Verona, Italy, who so apparently loved fish that they would come to the water's surface to kiss his hands. His name was Gualfardo. We are told of him in a popular hagiography written a century before Francis lived.[5] But the early commentators made it clear that Francis's love of God began through simple awareness of the wide world. Plants, animals, and perhaps fungi were part of that awareness.

The Conformity by Bartolomew of Pisa, one early text, puts it this way: "The first sign of the love of God is given when someone thinks frequently about God. For the power of love makes him always think of the one he loves. . . . This was evident in blessed Francis, who 'whether walking or sitting, working or resting,' was thinking constantly of God . . . the *Major Legend* says."[6] Here Bartolomew quotes the famous biography of Francis by Bonaventure. In this and other biographies, we meet Francis walking around in the woods dreamily, or walking on the long lonely roads of Umbria looking at birds and considering the goats in the fields, or doing nothing notable at all, and in doing so, what he pondered he was also paying attention to and loving.

Religious traditions are full of these quiet practices in ways that often go unnoticed or unappreciated. A century before Francis, the famous reforming monk Bernard of Clairvaux said, "You will find something more in woods than in books. Trees and stones will teach you that which you can never learn from masters." Judaism is also rich with teachings about how one learns from wandering in the wilderness. For Christians, at least since the late medieval mystics, the chief wandering metaphor has been the desert; in Judaism, it is wilderness; neither word nor place feels welcoming, at first, but for those who walk within those landscapes, they are meant to be.

These are places we were made to walk in. A Franciscan, surely every human being, learns about themselves and the world they inhabit by walking into woods and deserts and beside running water.

Many of us even love the desert, love the deep woods, when we're slightly lost in them. The word in Hebrew for "wilderness," *badmidbar*, interestingly is also sometimes translated as "desert." In the Midrash, the rabbis summarize the purpose of the ancient Israelites' wandering this way: "Anyone who does not make themselves ownerless like the wilderness cannot acquire the wisdom and the Torah." I love that. In both wilderness and desert, "there is something about the expansiveness and simplicity of the environment that makes people contemplative and aware of their insignificance." Psychologist Erich Fromm wrote, "The desert is not a home. There are no cities. There is no property. It is the place of nomads who have that which they need, and all that they need is life's essentials, not belongings. . . . Life in the desert is preparation for a life of freedom." Again, the Midrash says this, which reminds me of who I am as I walk: "God led them around in the desert for forty years. Said the Blessed Holy One: If I lead them the direct way, every person will take hold of his field and his vineyard, and will not engage in Torah. Instead I will lead them through the wilderness, and they will eat the manna and drink the water of the [miraculous] well, and the Torah will settle in their bodies."[7]

We don't know if Francis met with people from Jewish communities or even heard the word "midrash," but he understood this wisdom from his own tradition and in the practices that he cultivated. Everything he met in his pondering walks spoke of the miraculous earth and the descant of the wren. They were there—and are there, still—for each person who is willing to pay attention and listen.

Chapter 11

FIND YOUR COURAGE

There's an episode in Francis's life that you probably have not heard before because it isn't understood as miraculous, and it doesn't make anyone feel particularly good. It involves Francis and the best friend who betrayed him.

We saw that many unwelcome things transpired during the time Francis journeyed to meet the sultan in Egypt. He took that journey ten years into his life as a friar, of living with a religious rule approved by the pope in Rome, with many spiritual brothers and sisters, preaching and traveling and sending off hundreds, then thousands, of his followers to start new branches of their spiritual reform around the world. What was so well established soon turned into schism. (See chapter 2.)

When he returned, much had changed at the home base in Assisi. (See chapters 7 and 9.) While he was away, the friars must have imagined, not unreasonably, that they would never see their founder again. Some of them also imagined that Francis had gone there with the intention of martyrdom. As the months went on with no word, what happened was what always seems to happen when a charismatic spiritual leader dies or moves on and those who are left behind have to try to continue. They find it difficult to carry that dynamic movement forward without that original charisma. So they turn to structures, new leaders, additional rules, and they begin to build their own institutions.

What was unique about Francis's situation was how his followers moved on before he himself "moved on." In the spring of 1220, he returned from Egypt and the Holy Land healthy and unharmed. Some of his friends were shocked to see him again, walking through the door as news of the victorious sultan traveled, ending the horrific Fifth Crusade, sending Western forces running away from the Holy Land, back home.

And Francis returned to Assisi to find that the spirit of his movement had been compromised, shifted, and steered into places contrary to what the Friars Minor were supposed to be about. The new self-proclaimed "cardinal protector" of the Franciscans had begun to exercise favors—that Francis never would have requested and didn't want—on behalf of the entire movement. By the time of the general chapter meeting of all the friars, just after Francis's return, this cardinal protector named Ugolino was the one in charge. This announcement was quickly followed by Francis stepping down from leadership.

Which returns us to the episode from Francis's life that you probably haven't heard. There was a friar whom Francis had appointed as his vicar and as vicar of the order itself. His name was Brother Elias, whom we met briefly in an earlier chapter. He was the special friend with whom Francis often went to pray in caves, in the early days. He was one of Francis's closest friends and his confidant.

Soon after Francis returned and resigned his leadership, Elias graduated from vicar to minister-general. Not long after, Elias veered into a path of corruption and greed. Overcome with a desire for power and influence, his faith went sharp and bitter like milk turned sour. It was as if all those years by Francis's side were as nothing to him anymore. We don't know how much of this Francis observed, because he didn't speak of it per se. But we know that Francis never imagined the world as a place without evil. As Aleksandr Solzhenitsyn said, the line between good and evil runs through the heart of every human being. Even in this time, Francis kept Elias close in hope of turning him back toward the good. He met with painful moments in his life that ran counter to the sweet images we usually have.

It was at this time, with disruption all around and his best friend corrupted by power, that Francis wrote a letter challenging leaders everywhere to remember the responsibilities they have before God. It wasn't in his nature to write public letters like this. He wasn't a confrontational person. And the older he became, the more he could be found on the introvert end of the introvert-extrovert scale. So this letter took courage.

"I am Brother Francis, your small, humble servant of God," he began, in his usual quiet fashion, quickly moving to what was essential: "We should all reflect and understand that our day of death is coming soon. . . . When that day of death comes, all that you believe is yours will be taken away from you. The punishments of hell are greater for those who were the most powerful and world-wise in this life," he wrote in words surely talking, first and foremost, to his friend.[1]

How intriguing Francis was, in how he combined such love and affection with such seriousness for life matters in relationships with his friends! For example, in the iconology of Francis, you'll often see him holding a human skull. There's a famous Caravaggio painting that depicts this, and an El Greco, and several Zurbarans. They are usually titled or described as "Saint Francis in Meditation." This connection to skulls doesn't reflect an actual carrying of skulls—quite the opposite; one doesn't sing French love songs *and* carry skulls. But because he was often reminding himself and others *Memento mori* (Remember you must die), in a sense, he carried that gravitas with him.

In this letter to people in power, he then built to a crescendo, saying, remember God and remember not to do anything to hinder those who are subject to you to do the same. But it is the courage to talk to anyone this way, especially a close friend, that catches my attention.

These moments in Francis's life go unnoticed—when he left his comfort zone to do what he felt he must do or must say.

In another story, from late in his life, Francis showed courage again as he began to speak about matters that were important to him, from the concerns of his heart, but that he knew would confuse and upset many who looked to him for guidance and authority. It was during this time that Francis wrote his famous "Canticle of the Creatures." Today we know it as a beautiful and innocent song to the created world, but in Francis's day, it was considered highly dangerous.

He lived in a time when the "lower" creatures of the world were only understood functionally. Cows and horses, and animals generally, were thought to exist only for human purposes. There was no grasping the interconnectivity of species and natural systems. The celestial objects of sun and moon and stars were mysterious things in the sky with no relationship to what happened on what human beings believed was their singularly meaningful planet, plain and simple. No one in Francis's day mused about the inherent value of the nonhuman.

But he began to see every aspect of the universe as somehow related. Just as he had learned as a young convert to refer to earlier exemplary Christians as saints, to whom he appealed in prayer and for prayer from beyond, Francis began toward the end of his life to see similar exemplars in the moon, as his "sister," and the sun, as his "brother." Where several years earlier, he'd begun preaching to birds along the roadside, talking to them as one might talk to equals, now he began to think of other creatures, too, as his siblings. Even death, which he imagined was coming sooner rather than later, became a sister to him. This was highly unusual talk for a living saint, a title that the people were already giving him.

In fact, to many it would have sounded heretical. Truly, by the standards of the time, it *was* heretical. This was three hundred years before Copernicus. The earth was still at the center of the universe, and humanity was its singular, prized possession. Even two hundred years after Francis, there were those who began to suggest that God and creation were not so separate (among them theologian and astronomer, Nicholas of Cusa), and they were suspected and accused of pantheism because of it.

The Bengali poet Rabindranath Tagore wrote this about a century ago:

We have heard of poets who begin by imitating others. Such a poet may write many poems. . . . They sound sweet, but do not strike us as original. . . . Before, he had been playing on pipes borrowed from others; they could not express all the tunes his heart wished to play. He could not imagine why he was unable to play what he wished. It was the fault of the pipe! Desperately searching here and there, he suddenly discovered that he has a musical instrument within his soul. . . . The joy of the man who has found his own words, and has learned to express himself in his own words, knows no bounds.[2]

This language precisely captures how I explain what happened with Francis.

First, listening to his heart, he found his authentic voice. Second, he drummed up the courage to speak it, which isn't easy to do.

He wrote these words into a world around him that was entirely hierarchical. Violence and threats decided who ruled and who didn't. Walls and weapons determined safety. And churches spoke a language of power that their faithful did not. But there were other sources in the Christian tradition that did not point to power and to human structures: A God who walks with his creations in a garden; a God who later becomes one of them to feel, see, taste, and experience human life; and a God who is a Mother as much as a Father—these were Francis's inspirations. He was like "the great shaman . . . [who] gathers up the whole tradition of the despairing group . . . with all the circumstances of their present sufferings, into a . . . vision on the spiritual plane."[3]

But perhaps none of these stories from Francis's life can match the courage shown by his truest friend, Clare, when she decided to leave behind the comfort of her home in the wealthy section of Assisi. She escaped to join Francis where he was staying, below the city. Her family had planned for her to be married and begged her to accept a suitor, one of many who hoped to marry her. But Clare wanted none of that. When she fled, it was to escape a domestic situation that most people felt envious of, but to Clare, it felt like confinement. She'd heard Francis preach and observed his way of life, and she wanted nothing but what he said was possible for someone seeking to know God and to be free.

After dark on the night of Palm Sunday in 1212, Clare sneaked out of her family home and made her way beyond the walls of the city toward the little camp where she knew she'd find Francis and the others. She had observed their way of life, and it inspired her. There were very few religious orders for women at that time, and they were all cloistered nuns—instead, Clare was drawn to the life of a friar.

Here comes Clare, Francis's friend.

What are we going to do with her?

She looks determined to join us.

Join us, how?

As one of the brothers?

Look, Francis is welcoming her. He's calling us all together.

Her first gesture upon arrival was to show her sincerity in joining that band, and she cut her hair. While pious chroniclers often make this into a religious act, there was no precedent for it. Did she cut it, or did Francis cut it? The chroniclers always portray Francis cutting it and Clare bowing her head submissively. But there was nothing submissive about what she did that night. The courage it took to leave the only life she had known was a courage that Francis understood.

Perhaps she cut off what early biographers call her "beautiful hair" that night as a rejection of everyone's expectations of her. She had discovered who she was. She was striking out on her own.

In each of these examples from the lives of Francis and Clare, what begins to bubble inside them builds into streams that then flow gently outward, irrigating the places and people around them. I think, in each case, the engine that moves those native spirit-fed springs is courage. And any one of us who wants to walk the Franciscan way has to find our own quiet resolution and daring.

"Courage is the most important of all the virtues because without courage, you can't practice any other virtue consistently," said Maya Angelou. It isn't easy, but it's essential if we're to have an impact in the world.

Chapter 12

PRAY WITH THE MOON

It is difficult to imagine Francis praying in the living room of a home. He wasn't one for quiet domestic spaces. There was no warming himself by the fireplace in a comfortable chair with a devotional book in his lap.

Francis was deliberately unkempt. He would sooner sleep outside than in a bed. In his "Testament," his most biographical writing, he said that most often he preferred to sleep in churches. He didn't mean the comfortable parish house or even the pews. There were no pews back then. Think stone floors. He also enjoyed sleeping under the stars at night.

In the maturity of his converted life, in combination with his deliberate outsider status in church and society, he became the "celestial wanderer" that we met in an earlier chapter.

For many in the time of Francis, it was a custom to walk at night. Leaving comforts of home and hearth, people would make a path out of town into plains, over hills, to experience the night air and contemplate the evening stars. These were meditative hours. The medieval German mystic Hildegard of Bingen, most remembered for images of the green lushness of God (*Viriditas* was the word she gave this, meaning "greenness") to describe a life of communion with God, also delighted in the generative powers of the nighttime. Writing fifty years before Francis, she had a vision for how the sun and moon work together, inspiring that kind of engagement in human beings: "Humans work during the day and sleep at night, as the sun operates in the two modes . . . above and below the earth: during the day it shines above the earth, and with its descent at night the earth above is darkened. Furthermore, as human flesh is revived in its weakness by the powers of the soul—for the soul sustains its flesh and blood lest they wane—so too the moon is rekindled from the fire of the sun whenever it wanes." She continues, "The moon," then, "is the sun's helper in illuminating the lower things."[1]

In this kind of engagement of the sun, moon, earth, and its creatures, and that *viriditas* of God, we also see Francis. Over and over he awakes and gets up in the middle of the night, walking into the woods. He speaks out loud to someone. He knocks with his fist on his heart, as if to wake it up. We are shown these scenes from his life only because one of his fellow friars—usually one of the youngest boy friars who has recently joined—is secretly following Francis in the dark, watching from behind a nearby bush.

These are unfamiliar scenes in the lives of a Christian saint. In religion, we're more accustomed to finding solitaries under the moon in Japanese Zen. Matsuo Bashō, the great haiku master, often praised the "dark moon" that inspired him. But Francis shares a similarity here, in the purposefulness of night-wandering. Both the haiku master and the saint wanted to be solitaries, and both spoke about the moon as a way of showing disregard for civilization.

Just as I didn't want to make too much of Francis and the images of him holding skulls, I also don't want to make overmuch of Francis brooding. Just as frequently, I imagine, Francis was winking at the moon, as Bashō was, and praising the moon to draw out a smile in others. Also from Japanese Buddhism, and contemporary with Francis in the thirteenth century, is a collection of renunciation and holy fool tales called *Senjūshō*. In some of these short accounts, a Zen practitioner hides in plain sight—practicing reclusion more than seclusion by being alone in the midst of others.

Even before he began to pray outside, Francis prayed alone and through the night. The first person to begin to imitate Francis's way of life was Bernard, an acquaintance in Assisi. He invited Francis, a young convert, to have dinner at his house and stay overnight. This sort of hospitality makes even more sense if you remember that Francis was usually sleeping outdoors or in ruined churches.

That night, Bernard eavesdropped on Francis, curious to see what he was doing in his room alone, as he had heard the sound of his voice. He found Francis wide awake in the dark, in prayer. Witnessing his sincerity, Bernard was convinced that the young man who had once followed his father everywhere in fancy clothes was now acting like a penitent with genuineness and humility. The following morning, Bernard asked to join him in prayer and repentance.

Without those hours of night, alone with God in the dark, Francis couldn't have lived the life he lived. Not only was the darkness an aid to meditation and a kind of detachment from the world; for Francis, the darkness was also a path of not-seeing and not-knowing by which a person who in the light could not see as well could meet the Holy One. This is what John of the Cross wrote about in one of his poems: "In the happy night, in secret, when no one saw me, and I couldn't see anyone or anything, without light or guide, there was only that which burned in my heart."[2]

Rumi used to sing, in his poems, of how our shadows serve us, how we need the dark as well as the light in ways we don't yet understand. We try to escape our darknesses, which never really works, like trying to outrun our shadows.[3]

Another poet, Petrarch, used to say that it was solitude that made an event like the stigmata in Francis possible. According to Petrarch, for certain people solitude could be transforming, as it clearly was for Francis.

Some early biographers focus on both the revelatory nature of those night hours as well as spiritual battles Francis faced. *The Versified Life of Saint Francis* has Francis in those abandoned churches and lonely places battling demons in "horrid battles." In part, that reflects a truth. We all have demons—either of our own making or put upon us—and fighting them is absolutely a battle. But then the anonymous poet of *The Versified Life* has Francis going into spiritual ecstasies and turns the night scenes into a focus on the miraculous stigmata:

> Praying at night, he could be seen away up in
> the air
> Above the ground to stand, with his hands
> extended like a cross,
> All about him a gleaming cloud . . .[4]

Among the artists who have tried to capture this is Giotto. In the twelfth fresco of the Upper Church of the Basilica in Assisi, his painting commonly referred to as "Ecstasy of Saint Francis" depicts four friars looking on, with the city at their backs and woods on the far side of the scene, as Francis is suspended by clouds, his arms held open wide and Christ from heaven making a sign of blessing.

Words may ultimately capture it best. Eloi Leclerc, a French Franciscan half a century ago wrote some beautiful meditations about Francis. In them, he imagined what Francis himself might say in those moments under a full moon: "If we but knew how to adore, we could travel through the world with the tranquility of the great rivers."[5]

I imagine deeply grounding reasons for night-time walks and praying under the moon. Like most people I know, I often don't really know how it is that I know God. And what I know about God, I cannot say for sure how I know it. But I've heard myself converse with God, or at least that which I think is God, and I have heard (maybe "heard" isn't the right way to put it) God's holy and quiet responses to me and in me. This is *Emmanuel*, "God with us." It is a way of knowing. Even as Emmanuel is passive it is real: we receive it as grace and gift.

An athlete will work hard knowing that by hard work she may be able to create opportunities to win. Maybe prayer works that way too. Francis's mysticism wasn't earned, but it came after a lot of time spent in practice, often in the night's darkness. Even Petrarch in the late Middle Ages saw two types of people: the one is led around by the busyness of work and family occupations, and the other taps into what people are made for—solitude—and so are not led around by the cares of the world. It was this idea, and others like it, that made Petrarch a bridge between Francis's era and the birth of Renaissance humanism.

Moon prayer formed Francis's vision of a world much larger than what human beings occupy. We are rightly passionate about the importance of every human life, but from Francis we see that this misses the bigger picture of what is happening in the universe, in which human life is only one tiny part.

During the recent pandemic, when entire countries effectively shut down for weeks on end in order to stop the spread of a deadly virus and save lives, I thought about the larger understanding of Francis. The shutdown of countries was as it should have been, but there were those who ignored the orders, revealing themselves to be like some of Francis's contemporaries: arrogant and frivolous people, believing that the world centered around their own interests rather than seeing the value and importance of human lives on a grander scale. Also during that time, I found myself observing geese on a lake, looking at my dog in the living room, and watching birds and squirrels building nests, asking these creatures what they thought of our pandemic crisis. All I felt I heard in response was a shrug.

Moonlight prayer is about perspective.

In those night hours, I see Francis praying over and over again in two distinct ways. Sometimes he is praying like a bird or a squirrel that takes a drink or eats a bite while standing near some slight commotion that threatens to derail the sanctity of the moment. The creature leans in or bends down for a moment, keeping one eye or ear always aware of the distraction or danger nearby. But one has to eat and drink. So, too, one has to pray. And then sometimes I see Francis praying like an owl or a heron that washes alone in a stream at night, splashing and relishing in the quiet dark water, without any sense whatsoever of being observed—or like the songbird that migrates at night when cooler and calmer atmospheric conditions make it easier to fly—as one who is almost entirely alone.

In those night hours, Francis knew himself, and he knew God within him. He spent so much time purposefully and sincerely in prayer that he was able to follow God's direction, often hearing God in his heart. At times, he heard God tell him not to go anywhere: his work was right where he was. Other times, he heard the call, *Go*.

Sometimes there were demons to battle and other struggles that only the light of the night could illuminate. Most of all, he gained perspective and listened.

Chapter 13

MAKE A BIG TABLE AND INVITE THE NEIGHBORS

Francis never seemed to eat alone. To be honest, he rarely even ate—and that was a problem—but when he did eat, it seemed to be an occasion for gathering. He knew that there was no better opportunity for fellowship than over a meal. The blessings of food were meant to be shared.

Like his understanding of the interconnectedness of all beings, he had a vision for food that was inclusive of every creature—of everyone capable of hunger.

Thich Nhat Hanh, the famous Vietnamese Buddhist teacher, has often said that the future Buddha will be the *sangha*, a Pali word and Buddhist term for "spiritual community." In other words, the positions of savior and great teacher may, in the future, not rest upon any one person. For those with a Christian understanding, this is relatable, since the "kingdom of God," preached by Jesus as coming soon, is something we now understand we're supposed to bring about rather than simply waiting for a returning Christ to deliver it. It's something that happens in community. In Judaism, a similar idea of redemption exists: we don't wait for a messiah, because it is up to us to bring about the messianic age, when the world around us will find healing.

For Francis, this began in the most rudimentary fashion, as he gathered stones to rebuild churches. This led to helping lepers find clean water to drink and bandages for their sores. He chose the living and actual over the future and potential. This is so simple and yet so difficult; it runs counter to everything most of us are taught—we are always aiming or preparing for the future—even if to do so is to run contrary to our instincts.

"God has to do with every living being but not with ideas," Martin Buber used to say. And, "One who truly goes out to meet the world goes out also to God."[1] We don't truly find God in books or in the subtlest theology. We don't find God in beautiful churches or soaring hymns. These are good things, no doubt, but God isn't necessarily in them. God is essentially in living things. If we want to truly meet God, we have to go out into the world and encounter the living. As Francis did.

His table was wide open. But again, he was not often at his table. In fact, he owned no table. He had no regular place to eat. Francis was more often a guest at someone else's table—and at those tables, he could be infuriating.

There are stories of Francis being invited to a lush spread in some wealthy Catholic home, perhaps even a bishop's, and he is so turned off by the array of food and the wealth that he decides to leave the table for a time (a long time) in order to do what his Rule tells him always to do: beg for his bread. His hosts eventually discover him outside and try to coax him back in. He must have been infuriating at those times.

Where has he gone? Dinner is about to be served.

He's out by the road, my lord.

Doing what?

It appears that he's begging from passersby.

He's begging in front of my home?

Yes. In fact . . .

In fact, what?!

In fact, my lord, it appears that he has removed a bowl from the table and is using it as his begging bowl.

Would you kindly ask him if he would like to rejoin us?

In the very first biography of the saint, written only two years after Francis's death, we're told that Francis sometimes craved food and fought those cravings for the sake of penance and poverty. Perhaps he was craving pork sausages and truffles, foods that people travel to Umbria to find today. He also occasionally ate food onto which he'd added ashes or cold water to remove the pleasures of taste. He seems to have often felt that he was to be denied pleasure—even as he encouraged everyone with hunger to gather around the table. He was also known to sleep sitting up and refuse a pillow, believing that all of these steps were necessary to be faithful to his calling.[2]

Usually, when he was at someone's table, on principle, he ate whatever was put in front of him, obeying the teaching of Christ to the disciples recorded in Luke's gospel: "Whenever you enter a town and its people welcome you, eat what is set before you" (10:8). Sometimes this caused a scandal because even during his lifetime he was known as a saint due to his special relationships with animals—for Francis and the Friars Minor, in respect for the creatures, rarely ate meat.

On one occasion, Francis was the guest of a Lombardy man. And while they sat at the table, a beggar came to the door asking for food. Francis quickly gifted him some of the cooked chicken on his plate. Another account tells us that he would often slide a piece of meat into his lap, to avoid eating it; so, in this instance, I'm sure he was more than eager to give that chicken away.

But that beggar was a doubter in disguise. It turned out it was all a stunt to test Francis. The following day the man who had been begging was in the audience when Francis preached in town. As Francis spoke, the man yelled out, "This is what this Francis is like, whom you honor as a saint. Look at this meat that he gave me last night when he was eating." The man held up his saved chicken. But just as he held it up, the chicken, the story goes, suddenly turned to a fish, and the man was ashamed. Later, however, the story also tells that fish turned back to chicken ("after the liar returned to his right mind").[3]

But he was no stranger to feast, as well as fast. For Francis, the Feast of the Nativity (Christmas Day) was the feast of all feasts. It was also one feast on which he and the friars ate meat. The way that his first biographer talks of Francis's enthusiasm for the Feast of the Nativity is so lush and physical as to be almost sensual: "[This was the day] when God was made a little child and hung on human breasts. [Francis] would kiss the images of the baby's limbs thinking of hunger, and the melting compassion of his heart toward the child also made him stammer sweet words as babies do. This name was to him like honey and honeycomb in his mouth."

Francis's vision for celebrating Christmas at the table is a vision for more than a meal. He saw a world turned upside down by the Child Jesus (that "name" which was so sweet in his mouth). One of his fellow friars, a soon-to-be canon lawyer no doubt, says to him one Christmas Day that happens to fall on a Friday, shouldn't we refrain from eating meat? This kind of suggestion increased as time went on, and many of his spiritual brothers wanted to make their life more ordered, more rigorous, more rule-bound. Francis tells him, "You sin, brother, when you call 'Friday' the day when 'unto us a Child is born.' I want even the walls to eat meat on that day, and if they cannot, at least on the outside they be rubbed with fat!"

Francis goes on to speak of the stomachs of the poor and hungry being filled by the rich on this day. He desires even lowly animals, oxen and donkeys, "to be spoiled with extra feed and hay." All should, at times, fast. All should, at times, share in abundance and eat well. And he remembers his sisters, the birds, saying, "If ever I speak with the Emperor, I will beg him to issue a general decree that all who can should throw wheat and grain along the roads, so that on the day of such a great solemnity the birds may have an abundance, especially our sisters the larks."[4]

The Feast of the Nativity for Francis presages the feast of feasts, his vision for the coming kingdom of God. He wants his table to be as big as possible. And he doesn't see a lush spread so much as he sees a table gathering everyone to share together, everyone being fed, and more than satisfied.

Chapter 14

BE A MOTHER

As I've noted before, people were already beginning to call him a saint before he died. In this time, this was common. People sought comfort in this life and hope in the next, and if they sensed a saint in their midst, they attached themselves to the hope and comfort that saints represented.

At the funerals of saintly figures, there could be crazy moments with fervent believers attempting to get at the body and remove a fragment of clothing or even a relic from the body itself. The more cynical, deluded, or con artists would remove a digit or something worse from another body and claim it had come from the corpus of a special saint. (This is how we ended up with four competing heads of Saint John the Baptist in Damascus, Rome, Amiens, and Munich.) It was this relics culture, and Francis's reputation in the final years of his life, that led Francis's friends to bury him secretly at night and in layers of rock beneath the altar of the new basilica they built to house his body.

That so many revered him may lead you to imagine Francis as a powerful and attractive figure, but of course he wasn't. There's an anecdote from the early days when a friar named Masseo—the same handsome brother who we saw begging beside Francis in an earlier chapter—was gently but persistently interrogating Francis, asking, Why him? "Why does the world all seem to run after you? You aren't good-looking. You don't know very much. You aren't of noble birth. So . . . why you?" The text in *The Little Flowers of St. Francis*, where this anecdote is found, says that Masseo was asking these questions to test Francis's humility (though this may be the attempt of an editor to interpret the scenes). I think Masseo genuinely could not yet see why so many people wanted to be near this man.

Here's how Francis responds: "God chooses the fools of the world to shame the wise."[1]

Why are you following him?

There's something different . . .

He's just another penance preacher.

Who needs another one of those?

But he rarely talks when he preaches . . .

Not only was Francis not good-looking, not noble, and not book smart, but he was not even an unambiguously straight male. Should this matter so much? Yes and no. Few people recognize how Francis embraced the side of himself that we usually associate with femininity: gentleness and care for others that he likens to a mother's love.

Francis praised these gifts in his fraternity of spiritual brothers, and cultivated them in himself, instructing all the men to take turns being mothers to each other. "Let them be as mothers" to the others, he said. And then, "Let the others be as children. Take turns caring for each other this way." This was in his "Rule for Hermitages," written for the friars who desired to be in small cohorts together in remote places, usually caves on the slopes of mountains in Umbria. To hike there today is to see how steep, how narrow, these places can be. God help the sleepwalker.

But these were temporary settings, as was every setting and situation for a Franciscan. These temporary hermitages in the caves were what we today would call retreats—sometimes for a Lenten period of forty days and nights, for example, a cohort would journey together both physically and spiritually. They would help each other, taking turns. What did mothers traditionally do? In the cohorts of four, two brothers would care for the other two brothers' physical needs. This was Francis's intention for showing how both caregiving and receiving care are marks of the life of faith. It also allowed for a true retreat, for each pair knew they would also be cared for.

What a blessing it can be to pray and meditate without having to care for one's own basic needs, for food and basic comfort. There's someone there who makes the coffee in the morning, who provides a meal when you're hungry, who makes sure that the place is safe and dry, who ensures you are not disturbed. Our "mothers" do these things for us—whether they are our biological mothers or not. I imagine that the two mother-brothers even tucked the two other brothers in at night. Here is the complete short text:

Any among us who desire to stay in religious hermitages should do so in numbers of three,

or, at the most, four. Two of these brothers should be "the mother" and two—or at
least one, "the sons." The two who are mothers should follow the life of Martha, and the
sons should follow the life of Mary. Each has
his own cell where he can pray in solitude and
go to sleep.

They should all recite Compline each day
right after sunset and then diligently remaining silent, recite their hours, rise for Matins,
and "seek first the kingdom of God and his
righteousness." They should also recite Prime
at the proper hour and then end their silence
after Terce, when the sons can once again go
to their mothers.

Then, if necessary, beg alms as poor little
ones who desire nothing but the love of God.
And be sure to recite Sext, None, and at the
right hour, Vespers.

Hermitage brothers may not allow anyone to enter or eat within their enclosures. The
brothers who are mothers should aim to stay
far away from others and to protect their sons
from all, so that they are never spoken to. And
the brothers who are sons should not talk with

anyone but their mothers, and with the minister or custodian of our order, whom they may visit whenever they need to.

Now, "sons" may occasionally take on the role of "mothers," as brothers take turns in these spiritual roles by mutual agreement. And at all times, everyone should aim to eagerly follow the details mentioned here.

Francis knew that it can be a blessing not just to receive a mother's love and care but to be a mother—to give selflessly in these ways—to someone, even or especially if that someone is not biologically yours.

Francis offers us so many lessons from these simple caring ways, if we practice them again with each other.

Even before he wrote his "Rule for Hermitages," he was known to have the warm, caregiving concern usually associated with a mother. In his first biography, Thomas of Celano on two occasions refers to Francis this way. The first scene goes like this:

Once while he was staying near the town of Greccio, a certain brother brought him a live rabbit caught in a trap. Seeing it, the most blessed man was moved with tenderness.

"Brother rabbit," he said, "come to me. Why did you let yourself get caught?" As soon as the brother holding it let go, the rabbit, without any prompting, took shelter with the holy man, as in a most secure place, resting in his bosom. After it had rested there for a little while, the holy father, caressing it with motherly affection, let it go, so that now free it would return to the woods.

The second instance is similar. Francis is traveling in the Marches region when he encounters a man with two lambs slung over his shoulder. The man is carrying the creatures to market. Celano uses language unusual for a hagiographer, intuitive and tender even in the writing: "When blessed Francis heard the bleating lambs, his innermost heart was touched and, drawing near, he touched them as a mother does with a crying child, showing his compassion."[2]

There were other moments, too, when Francis praised motherhood and asked that others be like a mother to him. When he first stepped down from leadership of the order, soon after returning from the Nile Delta and the meeting with the sultan, the second person to join him, Peter Catanii, Francis first asked to be vicar to all the brothers—a role he saw as leading as well as nurturing. But when Peter unexpectedly died only eighteen months later, in 1221, Francis asked that his other good friend, Elias, do the same. Elias became vicar of all the Franciscans, and then a few years later, he became the first minister-general. It was Elias, as you'll remember, who began to lust for power and influence, and it is he who buried Francis's body secretly, deep in that rock at the foundation of the basilica he was constructing. At least one scholar has argued that Francis and Elias were so lovingly connected, for a time, as to suggest that they were gay.[3]

Instructing Brother Elias, Francis asked him to be "a mother to himself [to Francis], and a father to the other brothers." Francis wanted and needed the love and attention that he knew, at least from his own experience, was difficult to come by in a father. He needed a mother, and he wanted to be that mother to others.

In another writing of his, "My First Recommendation to the Faithful," which often appears today as the prologue in copies of the Rule for Secular, or Third Order, Franciscans, Francis said, "We are mothers when we carry Christ in our hearts and bodies with a love that is godly and a conscience that is earnest, and when we give birth to Christ through our spiritual practice, as a shining example before all people."[4]

He was a mother also in the way that he welcomed Clare into the fraternity on that first night, when she escaped her family home and ran to the valley where Francis and the others were camped. There were no other women there. She was the first. Later accounts would come to refer to that night as Clare's "investiture," which is a term also used when the Queen of England creates a knight, but that first night in the valley outside the city was truly something new. For a brief time—perhaps just a day, perhaps several days—there seemed to be no distinction made between Clare and the other brothers. She was one of them, and that's what she wanted to be. What was a fraternity became, at least for a brief moment, a siblinghood.

Also, in later accounts of what happened that night and in paintings from centuries later, we see Clare dressed in a bridal gown as she's having her hair cut. The image of a religious taking on a vowed relationship, even wearing a wedding ring, speaks to marriage, but the image also reflects on her own beauty and her family's expectations that she would become engaged and get married, as was expected of young women. As Francis was not an unambiguously straight male, so

Clare was not an unambiguously straight female. She was bucking convention and turning society on its head. This is also why the men in her family followed her and tried to physically drag her away from the friars, though they didn't succeed. They were furious with Clare, and I'm sure they were no more accepting of who they believed Francis to be.

And then there was one other woman among those in his sphere. Less familiar than Clare in the life of Francis is the figure of Lady Jacoba. She was a wealthy widow who was drawn to the work and teachings of the little friar, and Francis allowed her into the all-male circle of his religious order on many occasions. We have stories of Francis's fellow friars being shocked to see a woman at the friary door and then Francis instructing them to let her in. Some accounts of Francis record him referring to her as "Brother Jacoba."

All these accounts are reminders of what is more important than fulfilling society's expectations based on gender and often-gendered roles. Loving and caring for each other matters, and Francis shows ways in which everyone can mother others—in family relationships, in friendship, in spiritual community, extending that care. He also calls for the humility of receiving that care, at times, with the simple humility of a child with a parent.

Chapter 15

USE WORDS CAREFULLY

Until quite recently, Francis was not the darling of the religious establishment. Let me explain.

Consider how his work began: thieving from his father, and then splitting from him, dramatically and publicly. Remember how he chose to rarely travel to Rome, seeming unconcerned about seeking advice or approval for what he was up to. The less the Roman curia is in your business, the better. And at the end of his life, he wrote in his "Testament" how "No one . . . showed me what I was supposed to do; but the Most High revealed to me that I should live according to the ways of the Gospel." Coming from a Roman Catholic friar, this is a curious remark: it seems to imply he did not rely on intermediaries (e.g., a priest, a confessor, a religious superior) to discern the will of God.

It is also a remark that emphasizes how he valued every human soul's unique relationship to itself, creation, and God. For centuries, people believed that some people were naturally endowed with greatness of soul, and the masses of ordinary people were driven by their appetites. This idea was as common in the works of the Greek philosopher Plato as it was in the sermons of the Christian Middle Ages. But for Francis, every soul was naturally designed and able to relate directly to its creator.

He preached this as well. If you read about the Franciscans and Dominicans in a textbook, you learn that they were "preaching orders." Their preaching wasn't what is familiar to many of us today. It wasn't even the sort of preaching that one reads about in books about the Middle Ages. Popular preachers from that era would summon an audience and often lecture them for an hour. Other sermons, such as Meister Eckhart's, were subtle theological discourses. Francis's preaching was exceedingly simple. Sometimes he preached in churches, but frequently a Franciscan sermon was talking in the fields with people while they worked, by the side of the road as they walked, and in the piazzas where crowds gathered at all times of day. By all accounts Francis's words were exceedingly ordinary, not the words of the philosophers or lecturing religious leaders.

The pope in Rome had given his approval for Francis and his brothers to speak because they said they would preach repentance. What leader wouldn't desire more repentant—meaning, more obedient—subjects? But I suspect the pope wouldn't have been as pleased with the full range of topics that interested Francis and Juniper, Angelo and Rufino.

There are no transcripts of those early sermons because I suspect they were not sermons at all. They were more like conversations. Francis and the others probably retold familiar parables of the Gospels, or popular verses from the Psalms, in ways that were picturesque and illustrative. The Prodigal Son. Lazarus and the Rich Man.

On one memorable occasion, Francis was asked to offer a message to the small group of women who had gathered around Clare. We are told that he was reluctant to be there, to preach to this audience, but he'd been specially requested to say something edifying to them. So he walked into the middle of the circle of women, sat down on the ground, and without saying a word began to pour ashes over his head. He said nothing but simply remained there, covered in soot. The women all stared back at him. Then, after a few minutes, Francis began to recite Psalm 51, which is also known as the ancient prayer *Miserere*, from its Latin beginning meaning "Have mercy." It goes like this:

> Have mercy on me, O God,
>   according to your steadfast love;
> according to your abundant mercy
>   blot out my transgressions.
> Wash me thoroughly from my iniquity,
>   and cleanse me from my sin.

> For I know my transgressions,
>   and my sin is ever before me.
> Against you, you alone, have I sinned,
>   and done what is evil in your sight,
> so that you are justified in your sentence
>   and blameless when you pass judgment.
> Indeed, I was born guilty,
>   a sinner when my mother conceived me.

> You desire truth in the inward being;
>   therefore teach me wisdom in my secret
>   heart.

I wonder if that's what he had prepared to say or do, or if it was a change born in the moment.

One of my favorite twentieth-century poets is Elizabeth Jennings. She lived in Oxford, England; was a troubled Catholic; and suffered from depression throughout her life. She once wrote to her publisher/friend, Michael Schmidt, "I will give you a very lofty analogy for poetry; it is like the Eucharist, words are spoken, a simple element is offered and the words *transform* that element."[1] From what we see, Francis took a similar view of words to Jennings's. Words mattered, and words made things happen. Also, according to Francis, fewer words usually are the best way to communicate the meaning you intend.

It was this perspective that also led Francis sometimes to be horrified by his own duplicity if he ever spoke words that were not true. There was one occasion when, because he was ill, he ate a full meal including meat, which as we saw in an earlier chapter friars rarely ate meat except on very special days. Or when physical frailty seemed to call for it. Sometime soon after this meal, his health and strength returned and, as Bonaventure tells it, Francis suddenly realized that he could easily eat well without anyone knowing about it. That troubled him because, for years, he had taught his followers to eat whatever was put in front of them and be grateful for it and to beg for scraps on street corners and be grateful for that too. Here he was eating well, even if just that once, and worse, no one may ever know.

He didn't want anyone to imagine that he was so spiritual. He suddenly felt that he was a glutton for having eaten well, despite the circumstances. So he sent a message into town asking people to gather in the piazza that faces the spot where criminals were routinely and publicly shamed, and he directed a few of his brothers to tie a cord around his neck, strip him of all clothes except underwear, and drag him to the criminals' block, from which he then would preach. "Those who had gathered were amazed at so great a spectacle," Bonaventure says with a sense of praise.[2] Spectacle indeed.

This understandably strikes us today as eccentric, even grotesque. There are other examples of this sort of thing as well. One early text tells of a time when Francis gave his cassock to an old woman who was pleading for his help, and Francis then felt good in himself ("vainglory" the text calls it) afterward. I imagine he felt good that he had been there at the right time to help the woman and also that he'd responded the way he did. God knows we don't always respond in the moment the way that we later wish we had. But this time, having these feelings, it says, at once "he confessed to those who were following him."[3]

This sensitivity to hypocrisy must have struck others as excessive and odd, as it strikes us that way today. This was when Francis was already being sainted by his own contemporaries. He was growing cautious of the attention. He was embarrassed by it.

He even preached to the birds believing that his words mattered. Crows are among those mentioned by name as having been there for that first "sermon." I wonder if Francis was bothered by their diet, which includes the dead and decomposing. I wonder what he thought of how crows also feed on the eggs and hatchlings of songbirds. I suspect he noticed these things. He noticed most everything. He probably even knew about crows what experts on crows have said, "Everything about them says, 'It's me. I'm here. This is my world, my place in the world, and don't you forget it.' They are the opposite of shyness, the antithesis of camouflage, the very embodiment of self-promotion."[4]

The crows in his congregation were not small and melodious, prepared as such to praise their Creator in the ways that we imagine lovelier, smaller birds doing so well. But they have their own ways of praising with their lives. As do reptiles, which the same early chronicler tells us become part of Francis's attention after that first preaching to creatures event. I suspect that he spoke to each species specifically, but why would his early chroniclers bother to record such things?

The dignity of each creature, and every person, was the focus of most of his early preaching. Dignity was to be discovered inside of each of us, the very root of a relationship with God who created us. Then, as Francis preached, that basic dignity became the starting place for responding to the Creator, who wants us to sing with praises and gratitude for life and to seek the more fruitful and abundant life of each other.

The littleness of the birds was part of their natural appeal for a Francis sermon. He wanted that littleness for himself and others. We are all supposed to be little, and to remain so. Henri Nouwen used to teach the Christian virtue of "downward mobility," which is perfectly in line with this. Nouwen himself left teaching at Harvard Divinity School to live in an intentional community for people with mental and physical disabilities, practicing what he was preaching. The very name of Francis's religious order was, deliberately, Friars Minor, or "Little Brothers"—something

Francis was constantly reminding them, especially when bishops or universities or the pope wanted to honor them. A friar minor was not to hold high ecclesiastical office. Francis had enough trouble with the brothers' desires to become priests. He said this was to keep "their feet upon the ground" and "to imitate the footprints of Christ's humility."[5]

His voice was described as "vibrant and soft, clear and sonorous." His words were described as "soothing, burning, and penetrating."[6] Even as he was a person of few words.

In one of his last writings called "Praises to God," he fills a long piece of parchment—which still exists today—with nouns he used to try to define who he knew in the one "holy, Lord, the only God." Francis is writing directly to the Divine, saying "You are wisdom. You are . . . beauty . . . rest . . . justice . . . sweetness. You are hope."[7] And so on. It is said that he composed this as he walked down the mountain La Verna after the forty-day fast when he experienced God in Christ physically in his own flesh.

His preaching remained always rooted in experience, even when it consisted of few or no words. And he would, until the end, return to the same themes over and over again, beginning with turning one's life around.

Turning around began for him with action more than words. At the end of the first paragraph of "The Testament," that very late summary of writings of his to which I've referred already on a few occasions, Francis finishes describing what happened in him when God helped him to see the human face of the leper for the first time, describing the sweetness that came over his soul. Then abruptly, Francis concludes, "I got up and left the world."

He says it as if he walked into the next room. Or perhaps truer to who he was would be to say that he stood up and went outside, never to return.

Boom. He turned completely around. He started on a new path.

As we try to walk on the Francis way today, there's a clear call and a fine balance. There is an ancient Christian teaching of Saint Augustine that "there can be no justice without love," and then there is the way in which the professor and social activist bell hooks has more recently, profoundly and correctly, turned it around: "There can be no love without justice."[8] Without basic rights for all, to say that there's love is nonsense. An active turning around is essential. We need to start on a new path before we can rightly say that we have begun on that path.

In that final "Testament" of Francis's, he reminded his fellow friars of what was most essential. For example, every person who came and found him, wanting to live the way Francis was living, gave away their belongings to the poor. Every one of them lived simply. They agreed to work diligently. Each one was happy to live with less. They would pray the divine office. These humble offerings were a path begun in love and continued in love and justice. In summary, Francis says, "We were simple and subject to each other."[9]

Chapter 16

BEGIN TO DANCE

Anyone who tries to talk about God without at least some singing, dancing, or reciting poetry, is going to have a very dry mouth and rather dissatisfying conversations. As I mentioned in the introduction, I'm past the half-century mark as a human being and have begun to experience the way that life comes full circle, and you begin to wonder what is next. In Francis, I see a man whose singing and dancing and poetry increased the closer he felt himself coming to the end. Now I imagine that this is possible in my own life, when I never could have seen it before.

Achievement, adrenalin, passion, and ambition fuel early adulthood. I was full of those things, and still am, but when you pass the midpoint, other things set in as well. Song and dance and verse bubble inside even as we more often experience loss, and we are further removed from certainty.

There's a wonderful statue of Francis that sits in the courtyard of the Cathedral Basilica of St. Francis of Assisi in Santa Fe, New Mexico. See it someday, if you can. It stands life-size upon a slight pedestal and is called "Saint Francis of Assisi Dancing on Water." The bronze will bring a smile to your face. Francis's face is turned to the sky as he seems to attempt an arabesque with his left leg. His arms, covered in the giant sleeves of his cowl—which in monastic clothing symbolizes that we (our arms) do nothing without God's assistance—are made by the sculptor to look almost like an angel's wings.

Francis didn't literally dance on water, but he figuratively did.

His dancing was born from his own vulnerability, accepting it, and honoring the same in others, like heel turns, not hesitations. He never claimed to have the answers. But joy and song and poetry carried him. He would say that he did not know more often than he'd claim to know. And then he sang of all these things. He showed vulnerability also by admitting faults. At the end of his life, he even famously confessed to having done wrong by himself—he'd been unkind to "Brother Ass," as he called his own body. He hadn't sufficiently valued his own human life.

He danced, too, by giving of himself to others fearlessly. In one instance, a sick man asked Francis to help him with his bathing. The story goes like this: "Blessed Francis at once had water heated with some sweet-scented herbs, and undressing the leper began to wash him with his own hands, while another brother poured water over him. And as Francis washed and healed his body externally, so he cleansed his soul within."[1] Moments like these made it easier for him to dance.

Toward the end of his life, he prepared to face death without fear because he had already embraced how frail he was. Seven years earlier, he'd made his way to the land of the pharaohs and the Sphinx. To do that, he had to cross the sea, which may seem uneventful, but that's a peculiarity of our time. Up until about five hundred years ago, oceans were thought to be a chaotic remnant of the great flood that destroyed the world.[2] The Garden of Eden, after all, didn't have a sea, or any lake, or even a shoreline. There was only a chaotic expanse of water that God drew upon for the flood, and after it, oceans remained the most chaotic and unpredictable places on earth. But Francis traveled without fear. He had nothing to lose. This also made it easier for him to dance.

He lived unpredictably. If he'd been a musician, the members of his band would have had to wait and see what he was doing with his hands before knowing how to follow him. If he were a dancer in a troupe, he would have been the one improvising, trying something spontaneously new while the others tried to do likewise.

His dancing wasn't only figurative.

He was a juggler for God, a true song and dance man. As the medievalist G. G. Coulton once put it, "All through the thirteenth [century], we find an increasing flood of popular religious works, competing . . . directly with the ordinary minstrel. . . . St. Francis had told his disciples to be God's gleemen—*joculatores Dei*. He himself is recorded to have preached one of his most remarkable sermons from the text of a French love song: and one of his early disciples, Brother Henry of Pisa, resolved that 'the Devil should not have all the best tunes.'"[3]

Even once while standing before the pope in Rome, with cardinals of the church all around him, Francis began to dance. His first biographer explains the scene almost apologetically: "He was speaking with such fire of spirit that he could not contain himself for joy. As he brought forth the word from his mouth, he moved his feet as if dancing, not playfully but burning with the fire of divine love."[4]

He was obedient to God and to his faith. Today, obedience understandably troubles us. It is obedience that often keeps an abused person in the grip of an abuser. Obedience can also be a weapon, sometimes spiritualized, of those in power to keep those who are not firm in their grip. But you don't see that kind of obedience in Francis's life and teachings. He was obedient in the way the Desert Fathers and Mothers often taught. When some would praise obedience that's like the covering of the eyes of oxen so that they'll plod around a mill wheel forever without questioning, the desert teaching was that that's the devil. That's humiliation, devoid of God. There is instead an obedience to God and one's spiritual siblings, they said, that's done with eyes and ears and mouths wide open.

Obedience, juggling, unpredictability—all were part of his dance. And he encouraged others to dance with him.

It is common to see the life of a creative like Francis as one that begins with passion in childhood and then is gradually exhausted: the "fire" goes out, so to speak, perhaps from weariness or disappointment, since the world rarely understands creatives. I'll confess that I've run this ramble of interpretation even when it comes to the life of Francis in previous books: the narrative that he started his movement with fervor, eventually became disappointed, and then died relatively young after his battered body, and perhaps his spirit, were beaten up.

I no longer see him that way. I now see a person whose body was letting him down by his early forties but in whom the creativity was still firing. His dancing was no more evident than in the last two years of his life when he wrote the most singular teaching we have from any medieval saint: "The Canticle of the Creatures." In that song, he foreshadows and even inspires the era of scientific flourishing that was to come. One scientist, the English inventor of electrochemistry, said in a lecture in 1810, "Nothing is so fatal to the progress of the human mind as to suppose our views of science are ultimate, that there are no mysteries in nature."[5]

"The Canticle of the Creatures" shows the truth of that scientist's words. It of course wasn't science for Francis. Praising "Brother Sun" and "Sister Moon" was the vision of one who was free enough to see the world with simple attention. In the words of another poet, it was an instance of "a joyful, even ecstatic, obliteration of self in the act of attending."[6]

To glimpse what it must have looked like when Francis composed the "Canticle," or any of the songs the friars would sing, try to imagine this scene, which is retold in several of the early texts:

Francis sometimes did this: a sweet melody of the spirit bubbling up inside him would frequently become on the outside a French tune; the thread of a divine whisper which his ears heard secretly would break out in a French song.

Other times, picking up a stick from the ground and putting it over his left arm, he would draw another stick across it with his right hand like a bow on a viola or some other instrument. Performing all the right movements, he would sing in French about the Lord Jesus.

All of this dancing often ended in tears, and the cry of joy dissolved into compassion for Christ's suffering. Then he would sigh without stopping and sob without ceasing. Forgetful of what he was holding in his hands, he was caught up to heaven.[7]

At the top of this chapter, I mentioned the bronze sculpture called "Saint Francis Dancing on Water" in Santa Fe. There is another example of church art that speaks to these explorations. It is a vast wrap-around painted icon presentation of saints of all backgrounds and eras and cultures adorning the rotunda of St. Gregory of Nyssa Episcopal Church in San Francisco. Ninety people, four animals, stars, moons, suns, and Christ, are there, dancing. It is called "The Dancing Saints."

You should see it. Saint John Coltrane is dancing with his saxophone. Saint Francis is dancing with the Wolf of Gubbio. Thomas Merton, Malcolm X, Anne Frank, Anne Hutchison, Nicholas Black Elk, Cesar Chavez, Ella Fitzgerald, Christine de Pisan, Martin Luther, Mary Magdalene, Dante, Desmond Tutu, Bartolome de las Casas, Andrei Rublev, Mirabai, Pope John XXIII, and the Prophet Isaiah are all there, high-stepping, arm-in-arm.

Chapter 17

GO SIMPLY

I sometimes imagine Francis in conversation with a Zen master. It feels entirely plausible. For example, the Zen poet Dōgen Zenji lived in the same half-century, albeit across the world in Japan.

Dōgen inquires, *Where do you live?*

Francis says, *Here and there.*

What do you mean, here and there?

I move around a lot.

Why is that?

We don't build houses. We don't even plan tomorrow's menu.

Why not? Are you in a hurry?

Not exactly, but there's no telling where we should be next year, or tomorrow.

So you could simply settle into another home wherever you go tomorrow.

I don't think so. If I'm building, I'm unable to listen.

—

There's an antibourgeois sentiment in Francis, or at least that's what we might have called it a half-century ago. Today, I think we grasp it better in its sustainability. He lives lightly on the earth.

This simple, essential quality is lost in the legends. Read most books about the saint and you quickly find miracles and wondrous matters, but ask a Franciscan today to describe the Francis they know and simplicity of life will be among the first things they mention.

Miraculous saints became common and often extreme in visions and ecstasies and odd acts of piety in the time of Francis and especially after his passing. I've never seen a satisfactory explanation as to why. I suspect that religious people couldn't fathom a miraculous life without adding wonderment like fantasy and science fiction. For instance, Christina the Astonishing (that's how she was known), who died in Belgium in 1224, had apparently died once before, a half-century earlier, but climbed out of her coffin during her funeral mass. She was also known to leap into burning fires as a way of prayer and to free souls from purgatory. God had told her that purgatory would have no power over her, in this life or the next.

There was also the Cistercian nun, Saint Lutgard of Aywieres, one of Christina's friends. Lutgard's birth was only a year after Francis's, but she lived twenty years longer and the stories of her life were written just after her death. She was said, for instance, to have been thanked in person by the deceased Pope Innocent III—the Pope from whom Francis received permission to preach in 1209—for her beneficial prayers during his pontificate. She also asked for, and received, the heart of Christ. The Lord reached inside her and exchanged with her.

I don't find any of this particularly helpful. There was also a Franciscan Third Order saint, Angela of Foligno, who took Francis's instructions to care for lepers to ecstatic heights. She would clean their sores and occasionally eat one, holding it up and comparing it to a consecrated host.

It was in the half-century after Francis's death that some people began to claim that Francis often levitated three or four feet above the ground. Christina the Astonishing levitated to the ceiling of the church after she sat up in her coffin.

It was as if lives such as theirs or any life of faith they imagined for themselves couldn't be explained without mystical acrobatics.

There's no need to go to these places, to such lengths, to explain who Francis was. If you do go there, in fact, you begin to imagine that what he did was mostly irrelevant to real life. But that's not the impression you'll have if you read the early biographies of him, or better, if you read his own writings. He was extraordinary, yes, but he was also small, quiet, and human. This is important.

Francis's path to well-being and harmony is the opposite of how it is commonly understood today. He was free in ways largely unfamiliar to us. Today, freedom is generally understood to mean freedom from constraints, and we believe that removing obstacles is the surest path to happiness, peace, and pleasure in our lives. So, for instance, we look forward to Fridays when we'll be free from work. We might praise the freedom of leaving a fundamentalist tradition, or the freedom of not marrying, any freedom of not being "bound" to the rules of any form of obligation.

Francis's way is one of modest self-denial as the path to peace and fulfillment, and thus, joy and happiness. Freedom is to be found interiorly, not experienced exteriorly, and it is found by limiting desire and exposure to whatever might scatter our attention. This is part of the context we saw with Francis in the darkness of nighttime prayer. There are far fewer distractions at night. But also, reducing stimuli is a kind of self-denial. (See chapter 12.) And a simple life is one that cannot be easily blown off course by the winds of worldly concerns.

Both Francis and Clare "confined" themselves in these simple, easy ways, and by doing so, they found their freedom. Their "confinements" were not the ones that others wanted to place on them, and as a result, they were not "confinements" at all—but choices. A person with a different understanding of freedom would never be able to understand how it is possible to give up so much of what the world offers and yet be so free.

Francis began to learn this lesson when he journeyed from a life of worldly possibilities to one that was shorn of those desires, when he focused on seeing and doing what matters most. As the great Black scholar Cornel West has said, this is one of the most essential lessons that a person can learn, "To attend to the things that matter . . . substantial things, not superficial things."[1] If we don't relearn this, we will never find peace and happiness—real freedom—in our lifetimes.

This denial of the self—not to go every which way, not to follow every interesting thread, not to seek notoriety and fame—Julian of Norwich called "naughting." How countercultural it is to praise a path for living with a word that evokes images of finger-wag scolding.

Another late medieval Christian mystic, John of Ruysbroeck, spoke metaphorically of who he sought to meet in prayer, comparing God to "the dark stillness which always stands empty"—and depicting his own emptied self as "drunk with love and asleep" in that God.[2] That's Francis's and Clare's pleasure too, and it comes through an asceticism of simplicity.

Clare once advised a friend: "What you are doing, may you keep on doing and do not stop. But with swiftness, agility, and unswerving feet, may you go forward with joy and security knowing that you are on the path of wisdom and happiness. Believe nothing and agree with nothing that will turn you away from this commitment. Nothing should be allowed to prevent you from offering yourself to the Most High in the perfection to which the Spirit of God has called you."[3] This is for every person on the Franciscan path.

Self-denial combines with a carefree approach to living. This can be confusing at first. Being carefree doesn't mean not caring; it means not caring about what is of little importance. For Francis, such a list was long. His carefree list included, as we've seen, even what he would eat tomorrow, even where he might sleep tomorrow. Our lists will differ.

Langston Hughes began one of his early poems,

The rhythm of life
Is a jazz rhythm,
Honey.
The gods are laughing at us.[4]

God *is* laughing at us, if and as we organize our lives down to the fine details of where we will be in the next decade, or next year.

It's like the story of the man who dreamed of being rich and heard that treasure was to be discovered in a very special place, just waiting for the right person who is properly committed and prepared to go find it. So he travels a great distance and reads the instructions that he finds there, only to see that the instructions say, "Look under your own floor at home." There, it turns out, the treasure was all the time.

There is a way of knowing God that is much deeper and closer to us than any form of belief or conformity to the status quo. This knowledge is the awareness of our lives and our experiences as part of the life of God. This is why Francis begged his spiritual siblings to avoid studying theology if possible; it might easily get in the way of living with God.

The Swiss psychiatrist Carl Jung once wrote about this contrast in a letter to a friend: "People speak of *belief* when they have lost *knowledge*," he said. Much better, he then added, "The [person willing to be simple] doesn't *believe*, he *knows*, because the inner experience rightly means as much to him as the outer. . . . We have blotted it out with so-called 'spiritual development,' which means that we live by self-fabricated electric light and—to heighten the comedy—believe or don't believe in the sun."[5] This praise of the sun, instead of religiosity and theology, is what Francis knew as the way of peace, a way to overcome fear, and a way of grace.

Instead of theology and plans and administration, Francis wanted to know about love and hatred, passion and conflict, journey and joy—and he spent his life putting himself in the midst of these things. This is how he went out to meet with the Wolf of Gubbio that day, and why he came away knowing him as his sibling. It is easier to blame a wolf than to befriend a wolf. It is easier to see a wolf as something separate from who we are than to see ourselves in every wolf, and to acknowledge that we are all, at one time or another, wolves. And the problems that we often blame on wolves we may realize are problems for which we are in part responsible. History offers many instances and examples where people have blamed wolves—or tigers in Asia, or mountain lions in rocky places—for decimating a deer population, only to discover, after hunting those "predators" mercilessly, that human beings were to blame for the decimation all along.

For all these reasons, in all these ways, the lesson of Francis is to simply feed the wolf.

Francis was a little person who did small things that changed his world. He made the path a simple one. I meet Francis with the words of Svetlana Alexievich, the oral historian and recent Nobel Prize winner, who says, "I've always been drawn to this miniature expanse: one person, the individual. It's where everything really happens."[6]

ACKNOWLEDGMENTS

I want to thank Lil Copan, friend and colleague, for her shepherding of this project. Thank you, too, to Franciscan mentors Richard Rohr, Murray Bodo, and the late Jack Wintz, all OFM, and all my teachers.

To Frederic and Mary Ann Brussat, old and dear friends, and to those wrens last spring who kept me company many mornings by the lake, this book and its ways forward in an uncertain world is for you.

Thank you to Paraclete Press for permission to excerpt my translation of "The Rule for Hermitages" from *The Complete Francis of Assisi: His Life, the Complete Writings, and "The Little Flowers"* (Brewster, MA: Paraclete Press, 2015).

ABOUT THE AUTHOR

Jon M. Sweeney has been interviewed in print from the *Dallas Morning News* to *The Irish Catholic*, and on television for CBS *Saturday Morning*, Fox News, and public television's *Chicago Tonight*. His 2012 history, *The Pope Who Quit*, was optioned by HBO. He's also the author of thirty-plus other books, including the biographies *James Martin, SJ: In the Company of Jesus* and *Nicholas Black Elk: Medicine Man, Catechist, Saint*; *The Pope's Cat* fiction series for children; *St. Francis of Assisi: His Life, Teachings, and Practices*, with a foreword by Richard Rohr; *A Course in Desert Spirituality* by Thomas Merton; and *Meister Eckhart's Book of the Heart*, with coauthor Mark S. Burrows.

Jon's books on Franciscan spirituality have sold more than two hundred thousand copies. His *Francis of Assisi in His Own Words* and *The Complete Francis of Assisi* have become standard texts on many university and seminary campuses and with many Third Order Franciscan groups.

ABOUT THE AUTHOR

He speaks regularly at literary and religious conferences, retreat centers, and churches. He's Catholic and married to a rabbi; their interfaith marriage has been profiled in national media. Jon writes often for *America: The Jesuit Review* in the United States and *The Tablet* in the United Kingdom, and he's active on social media (Twitter @jonmsweeney; Facebook jonmsweeney; Instagram jonm.sweeney). He lives in Milwaukee with his wife and daughters and also has two grown children.

NOTES

Introduction

1 Ugolino, "The Deeds of Blessed Francis and His Companions," in *Francis of Assisi: Early Documents*, vol. 3, ed. Regis J. Armstrong, J. A. Wayne Hellmann, and William J. Short (Hyde Park, NY: New City Press, 2001), 492.

2 See Bartolomew of Pisa, *The Conformity*, in *Francis of Assisi: Early Documents*, vol. 4, bk. 1, ed. William J. Short, trans. Christopher Stace (Hyde Park, NY: New City Press, 2020), 110–11, 121.

Chapter 1

1 *The Complete Francis of Assisi: His Life, the Complete Writings, and "The Little Flowers,"* trans. and ed. Jon M. Sweeney (Brewster, MA: Paraclete, 2015), 217.

2 G. K. Chesterton, *St. Francis of Assisi* (New York: Image/Doubleday, 2001), 66.

3 Many of the translations in this book are the author's own. When a quote from Saint Francis, an early Franciscan source, or Meister Eckhart appears without an endnote, it is the author's own.

Chapter 2

1 *Francis of Assisi in His Own Words: The Essential Writings*, trans. and ann. Jon M. Sweeney, 2nd ed. (Brewster, MA: Paraclete, 2018), 114.

2 Edward Hoagland in *This Incomperable Lande: A Book of American Nature Writing*, ed. Thomas J. Lyon (New York: Penguin, 1989), 321.

3 Jim Dutcher and Jamie Dutcher, *The Wisdom of Wolves: Lessons from the Sawtooth Pack* (Washington, DC: National Geographic, 2018), 17.

Chapter 3

1 Patrick J. Geary, "Monastic Memory and the Mutation of the Year Thousand," in *Monks and Nuns, Saints and Outcasts: Religion in Medieval Society*, ed. Sharon Farmer and Barbara H. Rosenwein (Ithaca, NY: Cornell University Press, 2000), 19.

2 James Cowan, *Francis: A Saint's Way* (Liguori, MO: Liguori/Triumph, 2001), 37.

3 Mary Harvey Doyno, *The Lay Saint: Charity and Charismatic Authority in Medieval Italy, 1150–1350* (Ithaca, NY: Cornell University Press, 2019), 33.

4 Leprosy, or Hansen's disease, was common in the European Middle Ages. It was a chronic infection that caused skin lesions on the body and affected nerves. By the sixteenth century, leprosy waned, and experts are not sure why. As of the twentieth century, antibiotics became available, but leprosy still occurs.

5 Norman Davies, *Europe: A History* (New York: Oxford University Press, 1997), 279–80.

6 *Francis of Assisi: Early Documents*, vol. 2, ed. Regis J. Armstrong, J. A. Wayne Hellmann, and William J. Short (Hyde Park, NY: New City Press, 2000), 539.

7 Bartolomew, *Francis of Assisi: Early Documents*, vol. 4, bk. 2, 208.

Chapter 4

1 *Complete Francis of Assisi*, 208.

2 Bartolomew, *Francis of Assisi: Early Documents*, vol. 4, bk. 1, 237.

3 Augustine of Hippo, *Confessions*, trans. Owen Chadwick (New York: Oxford University Press, 1991), 10.27.38.

4 Quoted in Narayan Desai, *My Life Is My Message: Satyapath (1930–1930)*, vol. 3, trans. Tridip Suhrud (Hyderabad, India: Orient BlackSwan, 2009), 9.

5 *Francis of Assisi in His Own Words*, 25, 48 (although in the second instance I've altered my earlier translation to a new one here).

6 See Jon M. Sweeney, "The Use of Devotional Books in St. Francis's Day," in *The St. Francis Prayer Book* (Brewster, MA: Paraclete, 2004), 137–40.

7 See ch. 3 of "The Legend of Three Companions," an early text. This is my translation, as are many of the translations from early Franciscan sources in this book.

Chapter 5

1 Emily Dickinson, poem #165.

Chapter 6

1 Pope Francis, *Laudato Si'*, 2015, #95.

2 Luther Standing Bear, quoted in *Our Hearts Fell to the Ground: Plains Indian Views of How the West Was Lost* (New York: Bedford / St. Martin's, 1996), 125.

3 *Francis of Assisi in His Own Words*, 40.

4 Thomas of Celano, "The Life of Saint Francis," in *Francis of Assisi: Early Documents*, vol. 1, ed. Regis J. Armstrong, J. A. Wayne Hellmann, and William J. Short (Hyde Park, NY: New City Press, 1999), 234.

5 Celano, 250–51.

6 Celano, 250–51.

7 Emanuele Coccia, *The Life of Plants: A Metaphysics of Mixture* (Medford, MA: Polity, 2018), 99.

8 Rainer Maria Rilke, *Selected Poems*, ed. Robert Vilain (New York: Oxford University Press, 2011), xxi.

9 Wassily Kandinsky quoted in Fenton Johnson, *At the Center of All Beauty: Solitude and the Creative Life* (New York: Norton, 2020), 67.

10 Coccia, *Life of Plants*, 20.

Chapter 7

1 Mimlu Sen, *The Honey Gatherers: Travels with the Bauls, the Wandering Minstrels of India* (London: Rider, 2009), 5, 18.

2 Bartolomew, *Francis of Assisi: Early Documents*, vol. 4, bk. 2, 217.

3 Bartolomew, 217.

Chapter 8

1 Bartolomew, *Francis of Assisi: Early Documents*, vol. 4, bk. 1, 238.

Chapter 9

1 This quote and those that follow are from a thirteenth-century biographical account called "The Anonymous of Perugia." *Francis of Assisi: Early Documents*, vol. 2, 38.

2 See Italo Calvino, *Italian Folktales*, trans. George Martin (New York: Penguin Classics, 2000), 594–95.

3 Father Cuthbert, *The Capuchins: A Contribution to the History of the Counter-Reformation*, vol. 1 (London: Sheed and Ward, 1928), 19.

Chapter 10

1 From "Anonymous of Perugia," *Francis of Assisi: Early Documents*, vol. 2, 42.

2 Roger Tory Peterson, *A Field Guide to Western Birds* (Boston: Houghton Mifflin, 1961), 223.

3 Coccia, *Life of Plants*, 5.

4 Robin Wall Kimmerer, *Braiding Sweetgrass: Indigenous Wisdom, Scientific Knowledge and the Teachings of Plants* (Minneapolis: Milkweed Editions, 2015), 48.

5 Doyno, *Lay Saint*, 24.

6 Bartolomew, *Francis of Assisi: Early Documents*, vol. 4, bk. 1, 68.

7 "Anyone who does not make themselves . . ." from Bamidbar Rabbah 1:7; "There is something . . ." by Erica Brown; "The desert is not a home . . ." by Erich Fromm; and quotation from Midrash Tanhuma are all from a paper of the

Reconstructionist movement, "Why Was Torah Given in the Wilderness," available at https://tinyurl.com/y64k7jsg.

Chapter 11

1 See "Letter to Those Who Rule over People (1220)," *Complete Francis of Assisi*, 232–33.
2 *Rabindranath Tagore: Selected Writings on Literature and Language*, ed. Sisir Kumar Das and Sukanta Chaudhuri (New Delhi: Oxford India, 2001), 42. I have changed three words from their King James Bible–sounding originals (Tagore often translated his Bengali into English this way) to twenty-first-century equivalents.
3 Ted Hughes, *Shakespeare and the Goddess of Complete Being* (New York: Farrar, Straus and Giroux, 1992), 89.

Chapter 12

1 Saint Hildegard of Bingen, *The Book of Divine Works*, trans. Nathaniel M. Campbell (Washington, DC: Catholic University of America Press, 2018), 149, 88.
2 This is my paraphrase in prose of others' renderings in verse. For comparison, see *The Collected Works of St. John of the Cross*, trans. Kieran Kavanaugh and Otilio Rodriguez (Washington, DC: ICS, 1991), 359.
3 See Coleman Barks, trans., "Shadow and Light Source Both," in *The Soul of Rumi: A New Collection of Ecstatic Poems* (New York: HarperOne, 2002), 88.
4 *Francis of Assisi: Early Documents*, vol. 3, 102.
5 Eloi Leclerc, *Wisdom of the Poverello* (Chicago: Franciscan Herald, 1989), 79.

Chapter 13

1   Maurice Friedman, *My Friendship with Martin Buber* (Syracuse, NY: Syracuse University Press, 2020), 40; and from *I and Thou*, in *Kol Haneshamah: Shabbat Vehagim*, 3rd ed. (Wyncote, PA: Reconstructionist, 1996), 189.
2   See *Francis of Assisi: Early Documents*, vol. 1, 227.
3   *Francis of Assisi: Early Documents*, vol. 3, 50. For "slide a piece of meat into his lap," see *Francis of Assisi: Early Documents*, vol. 1, 392.
4   *Francis of Assisi: Early Documents*, vol. 2, 374–75.

Chapter 14

1   See "Brother Masseo Tests St. Francis's Humility," *Complete Francis of Assisi*, 282.
2   *Francis of Assisi: Early Documents*, vol. 1, 235, 249.
3   Kevin C. A. Elphick, "Gender Liminality in Franciscan Sources" (master's thesis, St. Bonaventure University, 1998). A copy may be found in their Franciscan Institute library. See also Elphick, "Brother Elias: Soulmate to Saint Francis of Assisi?," *Jesus in Love* (blog), October 3, 2013, https://tinyurl.com/yxaqpoa5.
4   *Complete Francis of Assisi*, 228.

Chapter 15

1   Elizabeth Jennings to Michael Schmidt, 1984, *Fifty Fifty: Carcanet's Jubilee in Letters*, ed. Robyn Marsack (Manchester, UK: Carcanet, 2019), 172. Her emphasis.
2   *Francis of Assisi: Early Documents*, vol. 2, 570.
3   *Francis of Assisi: Early Documents*, vol. 3, 307.
4   Candace Savage, *Crows* (Vancouver: Greystone, 2005), 12.

5 *Francis of Assisi: Early Documents*, vol. 4, bk. 2, 216.

6 Andre Vauchez, *Francis of Assisi: The Life and Afterlife of a Medieval Saint* (New Haven, CT: Yale University Press, 2013), 72–73.

7 See *Complete Francis of Assisi*, 238.

8 bell hooks, *All about Love: New Visions* (New York: William Morrow, 2018), 19.

9 See *Complete Francis of Assisi*, 250–53. The quotation is from p. 251.

Chapter 16

1 *Francis of Assisi: Early Documents*, vol. 4, bk. 2, 212.

2 This idea, and some other descriptions of medieval understandings of the sea, originated in Alain Corbin's *The Lure of the Sea*, trans. Jocelyn Phelps (New York: Penguin, 1994).

3 G. G. Coulton, *Medieval Panorama: The English Scene from Conquest to Reformation* (Cambridge: Cambridge University Press, 1938), 529.

4 *Francis of Assisi: Early Documents*, vol. 1, 245.

5 Humphry Davy, quoted in Richard Holmes, *The Age of Wonder: How the Romantic Generation Discovered the Beauty and Terror of Science* (London: HarperPress, 2009), xiii.

6 This is how a later poet, John Clare, is described by Geoffrey Summerfield, *John Clare: Selected Poems* (New York: Penguin, 2000), 22. I believe the phrase is perfect for Francis as well.

7 *Francis of Assisi: Early Documents*, vol. 3, 340.

Chapter 17

1 Cornel West, "The Historical Philosophy of W. E. B. Du Bois—Class 1" (lecture, Dartmouth College, Hanover, NH, Summer 2017). See the 9:40 mark at https://tinyurl.com/yxzkyemp.

2 John Ruusbroec, *The Spiritual Espousals and Other Works*, trans. James A. Wiseman (Mahwah, NJ: Paulist, 1985), 265, 267.

3 Saint Clare of Assisi to Agnes of Prague, in Jon M. Sweeney, *The St. Clare Prayer Book: Listening for God's Leading* (Brewster, MA: Paraclete, 2007), 59–60.

4 Langston Hughes, "Lenox Avenue: Midnight," 1926 poem, public domain.

5 Carl Jung to Heinrich Boltze, *C. G. Jung Letters: 1951–1961*, vol. 2, ed. Gerhard Adler and Aniela Jaffe, trans. R. F. C. Hull (London: Routledge and Kegan Paul, 1976), 5, adapted. I've substituted "the person willing to be simple," a roughly synonymous descriptive phrase for Jung's "naïve primitive."

6 Svetlana Alexievich, *Secondhand Time: The Last of the Soviets*, trans. Bela Shayevich (New York: Random House, 2017), 4.